COMING AROUND

COMING AROUND

*Parenting Lesbian, Gay, Bisexual
and Transgender Kids*

Anne Dohrenwend, PhD, ABPP

NEW HORIZON PRESS
Far Hills, New Jersey

Requests for permission should be addressed to:
New Horizon Press
P. O. Box 669
Far Hills, NJ 07931

Anne Dohrenwend, PhD, ABPP
Coming Around: Parenting Lesbian, Gay, Bisexual and Transgender Kids

Cover design: Robert Aulicino
Interior design: Scribe Inc.

Library of Congress Control Number: 2012932037

ISBN–13: 978–0–88282–393–5
New Horizon Press

Manufactured in the U. S. A.

16   15   14   13   12   1   2   3   4   5

*In memory of my father, Edward Dohrenwend,
who parented me with great love and ample wisdom.*

AUTHOR'S NOTE

Coming *Around* offers advice about parenting a gay child. In it, I have attempted to explain coming out as a psychological process that unfolds within the broader context of social and emotional maturation. It is important for parents to understand how oppression influences emotional development and how emotional development affects adjustment to sexual orientation. A broader understanding of development will also help you understand what your child needs from you for you both to cope best with his or her sexuality.

This book is largely geared toward coming out during the age of adolescence and young adulthood. I believe it will be useful for those with adult children who've come out later in life as well. Many of the struggles are the same, regardless of age. When the issues are different, I've tried to make those distinctions clear.

I delve into some of the religious beliefs which you and your child will probably confront. The anti-gay stances of some religions have impacted lesbians, gays, bisexuals, transgender and queer individuals (LGBTQs) of faith and shaped public attitudes toward homosexuality. For many, religious beliefs will be one barrier that stops you from accepting your child's sexual orientation. Religion may affect your child's self-acceptance as well. On closer inspection, I think you will discover that your beliefs allow for differences between you and your child and those differences need not and should not interfere with maintaining a loving parent-child relationship.

Throughout the text I have tried to indicate clearly whether something is based on scientific evidence, clinical experience or personal opinion. Please be aware that my sources are selected with great care. I only cite sources from peer-reviewed scientific journals, qualified experts and, on occasion, from well-regarded Web sites. I try to use updated references only. The social and political climate for LGBTQs has changed dramatically over the past decade. Research completed more than ten years ago does not accurately reflect those changes. When I rely on older research, it is because the scope or quality of the work has not been bettered.

This book is based on my research, personal experience, interviews and clients' real life experiences. In order to protect privacy, names have been changed and identifying characteristics have been altered except for contributing experts. For purposes of simplifying usage, the pronouns s/he and his/her are sometimes used interchangeably. The information contained herein is not meant to be a substitute for professional evaluation and therapy with mental health professionals.

At the time of writing this, I am fifty years old. It is a good age to be. I know who I am and I feel happy and at peace. I am married (in our fifteenth year) and we have a son. The joy he brings to me and my partner is beyond measure. He makes me want to be the best parent I can be.

There is no greater agony than bearing an untold story inside you.

MAYA ANGELOU

Contents

Introduction

"I'm gay." These few words, from child to parent, can transform the relationship. Whether that transformation results in a closer bond or a broken one is largely dependent on you, the parent.

As a parent, I know how you feel and how much you love your child. You picked up this book because you feel sad, angry or unsure of what to say and do now that you've learned that your son or daughter is gay. You know that your child's coming out and your response to it are important. You want to do the right thing. That says a lot about you. What you may not yet realize is that this challenging moment can lead to a better, more authentic parent-child relationship. This moment of risk and honesty is full of potential for both of you.

The first step in preserving your relationship with your son or daughter is self-exploration. Whether you've thought of homosexuality as acceptable or unacceptable in the past, your child's announcement requires that you re-explore the issue with greater depth and scope. None of us is immune to the cultural stigmatization of homosexuality. With greater self-awareness, you will be less likely to make statements that may inadvertently hurt your child. With insight, you will be more likely to offer sound, empathic advice.

You do not have to march in gay pride parades in order to be a good parent. Additionally, you need not change your religious affiliation nor reject deeply held beliefs. Disagreements about the nature of homosexuality will likely add tension to the relationship, especially during particular phases of your child's adjustment to his/her sexual orientation, but that tension doesn't have to tear apart the relationship. It is normal for children and parents to disagree. It is part of the natural process of maturation. It is also a generational reality. We do not live in the world of our parents and our children will not live in ours. There is, however, a right way to convey disagreement and a wrong way. Relationships that survive conflict do so because differences are conveyed with respect for boundaries, personal humility and a sense of perspective.

Be assured of one thing: Your child can live a full and happy life. If you have any doubt about this, I hope that reading this book will put your mind at ease. Some things that frighten you about your child being gay are no more real than monsters under the bed. When your child was little, you sent those monsters running with courage and logic. You can do the same now with your child's and your worries about homosexuality.

PART I

TEMPERING FIRST REACTIONS

Chapter 1

Taking a Generational Perspective

You were brought up in one world and you raise your child in another. This complicates parenting. Even if you try to keep up with this changing world, you can never see the world the way your child sees it. The Greek philosopher Heraclitus of Ephesus taught us: "You can never step in the same river twice." If you've ever tried to re-create a magical moment by returning to the same spot and reenacting the event, you know this is true. The place will have changed, if ever so slightly, and you will have changed, if ever so slightly, as well.

Think of all the dramatic shifts in lifestyle that have occurred over the last four decades. Middle class children born in the sixties or seventies didn't have cell phones, computers or electronic games. Parents located their children by calling neighbors via landlines or by shouting outside. Family life in this era was represented by the family on the popular television show *The Brady Bunch*. Jan could be jealous of her sister's popularity and Peter did a bit of sneaking behind his parents' backs, but drugs and sex were topics not addressed. In this era, stimulation was, well, much less stimulating. Superheroes Batman and Superman were about as violent as it got, at least until teenagers were old enough for R-rated movies. Though the world was not safer, it *seemed* safer back then. Bad things happened in American homes—incest, emotional abuse and violence—but they were not openly discussed. A child untouched by such tragedies was protected from the reality of their existence until s/he was much older.

There were gay men and women in these communities, but, most likely, they were in the closet. If people knew someone was gay, most likely they knew it through whispers and assumptions. The social penalties for coming out were much more severe a few decades ago and legal rights for homosexuals were virtually nonexistent. There was a host of negative feelings associated with homosexuality. Gay people were thought of as foreign, odd, incomprehensible, lost, shameful, disappointing and perverted. There were few public gay role models and, for the most part, homophobia went unchecked. If you grew up in this era, you were probably never exposed to anyone who lived, shamelessly, as an openly gay individual.

In many ways the world is like a rushing river in a constant state of change. If a person stepped into the river twenty years ago, in many societies homosexuality was unacceptable and life as a homosexual was inconsistent with success and happiness. If a person was gay, usually he or she hid it and the future would have appeared bleak or blank (impossible to envision). The idea of a gay couple living as a happy family, married and with children, was unimaginable.

Your child has stepped into friendlier waters. S/he was born into a world in which gays are visible. Gays have created a space in the world and have defined all manner of futures for themselves. Among the possibilities are professional success, marriage and parenthood. Most likely your child is growing up seeing gay people interact and win acceptance in mainstream media. Your child sees gay people smile, laugh and engage successfully with the world at large. S/he has watched gay people speak up for themselves and fight with dignity and grace against those who would deny them basic human rights. Not only does your child have multiple visions for the future, but also your child has words and a history to better understand and explain his or her own minority experience. When your child has questions, s/he has public resources, if not locally then online, that are ready and willing to answer those questions. There is no doubt that as your child matures, s/he will witness or has already witnessed a backlash against gay rights and that s/he will hear or has already heard anti-gay comments, but these attacks against gays are in the context of growing public acceptance.

Why is it important to consider generational differences? If you dread your child's lifestyle, it may be because you envision your gay child living in the world you lived in when you were young. But your child is not living in that world. Recognizing this will not only help lift the cloud of worry, but also help you be more open to your child's experience in the present. In addition, recognizing that our world is in constant change regarding the acceptance of homosexuality will help to make you more open-minded about homosexuality.

When you were growing up you may have engaged in a generational battle with your parents. Perhaps it was over something small, like wearing jeans to church or synagogue, getting an earring or coloring your hair. Or it may have been about something big, like living with someone before marriage or moving across the country. At the time, you might have had the feeling that your parents wouldn't or couldn't accept change. They didn't recognize that what you wanted was within the range of normal and acceptable by the standards of your era. You wished that they would just try to see things from your perspective. Now it's time for you to see things from your child's perspective. Then it was about your life. Now it is about your child's life.

Parents with children of all ages, including adult children, may be reading this book. Your child may be telling you of his or her sexual orientation as a teenager or expressing his or her feelings even earlier. Or your child may have come out later in life, in his or her forties, for instance, and his or her perception of opportunities for homosexuals as well as his or her internalized homophobia may reflect the more limiting period during which s/he grew up. In addition, some current teens may reside in school districts and communities that disparage gay-positive influences and bar gay-friendly organizations. If this is the case, your child's perceptions of homosexuality may be as negative as those of someone from the era when homosexuality was taboo. Both my experience counseling and my research have shown that the sooner your child has contact with gay-positive people and institutions, the sooner the child will be able to question and discard any shame s/he may feel.

····························

Chapter 2

What Is LGBTQ?

LGBTQ (also initialized GLBTQ) stands for lesbian, gay, bisexual, transgender and queer. Over the years, the term *gay* has come to be used generically to mean anyone who is non-heterosexual. Throughout this book I use the term *gay* in this broad manner. *Lesbians* are women who are physically and emotionally attracted to women, *gays* are men who are physically and emotionally attracted to men and *bisexuals* are individuals who are physically and emotionally attracted to both men and women. *Transgender* people are those whose self-described genders do not match their physiology. Individuals who identify as *queer* reject all traditional gender labels and the heteronormativity of conventional society.

While lesbian, gay and bisexual refer to sexual orientation, transgender individuals experience an enduring conflict between internalized gender and biological reality. Though anatomically male, *she* feels female. Though anatomically female, *he* feels male. Many transgender individuals adjust their external presentation, hair, clothing, etc., to correspond with their felt gender. This is called cross-dressing. Transsexual behavior and cross-dressing can serve as a step toward transgender identity acceptance. It's a kind of "coming out." However, cross-dressing is not always a sign of transgender identity. Some people cross-dress for reasons other than being transgender, such as for theatrical performances, for gender experimentation, to make a political statement or because it appeals to their fashion sense.

People often confuse sexual orientation with gender identity. Sexual orientation is about the gender to whom one is attracted: men, women or both. Gender identity has to do with one's internal experience of being male or female. Some conceive gender as neither male nor female but instead as a range of gender-based sensations. A person may feel female in some circumstances but retain a reservoir of maleness for other situations. Gender is confusing because culture confounds attempts to define it. What is it to be feminine or masculine? In one culture, clothing may define what is feminine and in another, it is the ability to provide food for one's family. It is possible to feel entirely female and not particularly feminine. Likewise, it's possible to feel at odds with masculine stereotypes but feel very male.

Gender nonconformity is behavior or appearance that violates gender expectations. Gender nonconformity may or may not be something done in a conscious effort to bend gender rules. Some people are perceived as gender-nonconforming because of size, voice, musculature or interests. Other people consciously counter social expectations of their biological genders, such as a man who wears eye makeup.

Because of its growing use, it's also important to understand the meaning of *queer*. If you're a baby boomer like me, you probably wince at the word, but *queer* has been reclaimed by today's generation. When people of a minority group use with pride a reference term formerly used to shame them, it is called *reclaiming*. Reclaimed words take on deeper meanings than their original pejorative connotations. Those who refer to their sexual orientations as queer reject traditional labels of heterosexual, homosexual and bisexual. They see such labels as limited and limiting, because they are majority conceptions shaped by majority biases and mores. There is a substantial body of queer research that favors a broader conceptualization of sexual orientation and gender identity. While this type of research is still largely marginalized, the detoxified use of *queer* appears to be breaking through into the mainstream, such as in the television show *Queer Eye for the Straight Guy*.

Let your child define him or herself and adopt your child's language when referring to his or her sexual or gender orientation. Don't make the assumption that because your child is gay that s/he is unhappy or uncomfortable with his or her gender. If your child is transgender, don't make assumptions about sexual orientation. If you grew up in a time when words like *gay* and *queer* were reserved for gay-bashing, it may be difficult for you to utter them. Remember, your child is from a different era and s/he has the right to name his or her experience. If you have to, drive around in your car with the windows shut saying "queer" and "gay" as many times as necessary until they become just words.

You might wonder, *Why the big fuss over labels?*

The majority will often apply derogatory names to a minority group or degrade the minority's natural name(s). When a minority group is beaten down for a long time, individuals within the group internalize the majority's negative feelings and believe themselves to be inferior. In essence, the minority identity and its names are poisoned by the negative attitudes of the majority and that poison seeps into its people. A group that accepts its inferiority will be treated as inferior. Silence and invisibility ensure this. The minority group reasserts itself by throwing off imposed labels, reclaiming labels that have been tarnished and engaging in the process of rediscovering identity. I say this is a process, because rediscovering identity is complex, especially when one's identity has been bruised and battered, sometimes beyond recognition.

There will come a time when labeling one's sexual orientation will be out of vogue. Whether one is homosexual or heterosexual will carry no more importance than being brunette or blond. That day will be possible, because attacks against homosexuals will end. There will be no reason for gays to fight for their good name, because homosexuality will have thrown off any negative connotation. On that day, gay rights will be human rights and human rights will be gay rights. Until then, labels remain important. Analysis and debate over gays' identity and over definition of that identity is the only way to detect and remove the poison of injected inferiority. Asserting themselves is the only way to defeat those who might still attempt to demean gays or limit their rights.

....

Chapter 3

First Reactions

Homophobia is part of our social indoctrination. Whether you're gay or straight, liberal or conservative, most of us were brought up to think that being gay is abnormal. We all have a tendency to be homophobic. Even gay, lesbian, bisexual, transgender and queer people can be homophobic. In fact, most LGBTQs believe, to some degree, the bad things said about them simply because those statements have been said so often by so many. We call this internalized homophobia. In this chapter we will discuss the varied reactions parents may have to their child's coming out, how the homophobic societal indoctrination can affect reactions and how you can give your child the support s/he needs.

IF YOU ARE LIBERAL

Although you have always considered yourself liberal, when your child expresses that s/he is gay, you may experience a mixture of emotional reactions and intense feelings, including:

- Shock: But she dated so many guys!
- Guilt: If I were a good parent he would have confided in me sooner.

- Disappointment and sadness: I really wanted grandchildren.
- Shame: I'm having ugly thoughts and feelings about homosexuality.
- Fear: I don't want my child to be ostracized.
- Anger: The world isn't fair to gays.

Perhaps in the past you have considered yourself impervious to stereotypic thoughts about homosexuals and yet those are the very thoughts that keep coming to mind. You feel guilty, but you can't seem to block them out. Don't be too hard on yourself.

Resist the urge to turn away from ugly thoughts about homosexuality. Frightening and unhealthy thoughts thrive in the dark where they cannot be examined. Homophobic thoughts are no exception. If you want to disarm homophobia, find out where it hides and bring it into the light. One of best places to look for homophobia is to examine your first reactions upon hearing that your child is gay.

When my partner first told her parents that she was gay, they were, understandably, shocked. There was no evidence of past attraction to young women and plenty of evidence of attraction to young men. In so many ways she was quintessentially heterosexual; she was even a cheerleader and a homecoming queen. Homecoming queens can't be gay! As it turns out, stereotypes are misleading. Football players, cheerleaders and homecoming queens are just as likely to be gay as anybody else.

Early sexual behavior can be equally misleading. It is a poor predictor of sexual identity. Most lesbians and gays report having had intimate relationships with the opposite sex. Perhaps this is due to efforts to suppress homosexual urges and comply with social expectations of heterosexuality. On the other hand, it may reflect a general tendency for sexual experimentation. Similarly, many heterosexuals report having had sexual experiences with same-sex partners at some point in their lives.[1]

For some of you, the shock of discovering your child is gay is complicated by the fact that s/he wouldn't or still won't talk about it or even lied about it, perhaps for years. You don't know whether to blame your child for not trusting you or to blame yourself for not being perceived as trustworthy. You examine your memories over and over in an effort to recall anything that suggested your child was gay.

Maybe pieces of conversations come to mind, hints and more than hints, and you tell yourself you should have known.

It is time to ease up on the self-blame. It took your son or daughter time to come around to the idea that s/he is gay. Your child was the first to know and s/he got a head start on you on adjusting to the fact. Even if you considered the possibility that your child was gay, confronting him or her with that perception might have backfired. When a child is not yet ready to accept his or her sexual orientation, confrontation can result in further withdrawal. What's important now is to open the gates of communication so you can talk openly.

What if your child is angry at you? Your child says s/he tried to tell you but you didn't listen. What if s/he is right? There are many ways not to hear. Can you remember a time when your child started talking about his sexuality and you changed the subject or you said nothing and he never brought it up again? Maybe she began talking about a special friend and you made a joke or said something that shut her down. If so, her anger now is a shield. Your child doesn't want to be disappointed again. Guilt serves one purpose: it motivates us to change course. Once the course is changed, continued guilt is unhelpful. You can diffuse your son or daughter's anger by acknowledging past mistakes and by displaying a fearless alacrity for honest and candid discussions about homosexuality.

Maybe your child is not the angry one; maybe you're angry with her, because you feel disappointed. Disappointment is tied to expectations. Without expectations, there would be no disappointment. There are times when I fantasize about my son's future. In my mind's eye, I picture him as a man. He is kind and confident. He stands with his shoulders back and his head held high. And why not? He can do just about anything. In my mind, one minute he is collecting his diploma and the next he is performing at a concert. When he's not succeeding at work, he is home with his spouse and his baby. Yes, I can see him clearly, his brown eyes fixed on the cooing baby resting in the crook of his arm.

Is it right for me to tell my son about my dreams for him? Isn't that intrusive and overbearing? Doesn't it impose undo pressure on him? I have had a life full of choices and, for the most part, I've had the luxury to make them freely. My son deserves the same. On the other hand, a parent cannot lead without setting a course. While I will never tell my child what profession to choose, I will instill in him the expectation that he will go to college. While I will not tell him to have children, I do comment, as he rocks his baby doll, that he shows signs of being a good daddy. As my son enters early adulthood, he will begin to evaluate the course upon which his parents have set him. As he matures, he will decide if that course is right for him. When that time comes, the most important thing I can do is recognize where I end and where he begins and to keep my dreams out of his way.

Respecting your teen or adult child's life decisions isn't always easy, particularly if you fear that the decisions will cost him or her, one way or another. You may fear that life as a gay man or woman will offer less than life as a heterosexual. Many parents of gay children worry that their children will be cut off from a litany of opportunities, including the wonders of marriage and of raising children. There was a time when these fears were warranted, but now there are more options. If s/he chooses, your child can marry and be a parent. There are several states that protect gay marriage and respect the adoption rights of gay citizens.

If you take away only one truth from this book, make it this one: The greatest barriers to happiness that your son or daughter will face will be self-imposed.

IF YOU ARE CONSERVATIVE

Parents who are socially, politically and religiously conservative will usually have a more difficult time accepting and coping with a child coming out as gay.

- Shock: Homosexuality was never an option.
- Disappointment: Is my child doing something immoral?
- Guilt: I must have done something wrong as a parent.
- Shame: My child and I will be ostracized.
- Fear: I don't want my child to lose his/her relationship with God.
- Anger: I think homosexuality is a choice and this choice hurts me.

If, while out for a walk, you turn around and see a truck grille bearing down on you, your brain rushes a message to all corners of your body telling it to fight or flee. Almost instantaneously, your heart begins pumping harder, your breath quickens, your muscles tense. If the threat is a truck, these physiological changes will enhance your chance of jumping clear of disaster. Unfortunately, your brain reacts to all perceived threats in the same manner, even though all threats are not alike. A severe emotional shock can set in motion the very same physiological reactions as facing an oncoming vehicle. When that happens, a person reacts defensively.

If you believe that being gay is abnormal, a perversion or a sin, it was most likely a terrible shock to hear your child say that s/he is gay. It might have felt as if you'd been sucker punched. It might have seemed as if, in a very real way, the life of your child was under threat. At times like this, parents don't think; they react. If you reacted with a fight posture, you may have said something you later thought was unkind or even cruel. You might have attacked homosexuals and, in doing so, attacked your child. If your reaction was to flee, you might have changed the subject, been dismissive or literally fled from the room. Given your beliefs about homosexuality, your reactions were normal. It's what the body does. But what is normal isn't always what is best. The brain does not always perceive the world accurately.

You need time to evaluate your perceptions. You need to find a way to cool down, to slow down. Get out of the defensive mode and into the thinking mode. Stop reacting and start responding. Regardless of your beliefs about homosexuality, acting defensively at this moment will drive a wedge between you and your child. If you regret your first reaction to your child's disclosure of his or her sexual orientation, tell your child that you are sorry, that you were shocked and that you need time to think. Tell your son or daughter that you won't run away again and that you'll work it out together.

Meanwhile, you owe it to your child to learn more about homosexuality. Given your beliefs, it is unlikely that you have close friends who are gay. Limited exposure to gays has left you to rely solely on stereotypes. You need to get beyond stereotypes. Learning more about the LGBTQ community may not change your fundamental beliefs about the nature of homosexuality, but it may result in reducing or eliminating some of your fears.

I am openly gay at my place of work, but most clients who are referred to me for therapy are unaware of my sexual orientation and my position on homosexuality. Unless told otherwise, most people assume I'm heterosexual. As a result, I hear a lot of unfiltered thoughts and feelings about homosexuals. There was a time in my life when some of the things I heard upset me, even rendered me ineffective as a therapist due to my own defensive reactions, but I am in a different place now. I'm not without feelings, but I am less likely to let someone else's opinion define me. Ultimately, you want your child to be resilient to homophobic remarks and to have a healthy self-esteem. Even if you are against homosexuality, you can probably agree that healthy decisions can't be made in a context of fear or self-loathing. Only when self-esteem is intact is a person able to make sound, sensible decisions that promote success and health.

If you disapprove of homosexuality, your child has probably hidden his or her sexuality for some time. S/he may have withheld this from you out of fear of being disowned by you or of losing your love and respect. As your son or daughter, your child may share many of your values including the belief that homosexuality is not acceptable. If this is the case, then your child has probably tried his or her best to ignore or rebuke his or her sexual feelings in the hope that s/he could make them go away. Telling you now is an act of courage and a leap of faith. No adolescent or young man or woman wants to discuss sexuality with his or her parents. It is a time when children usually start defining adult boundaries with parents and privacy with regard to sexual behavior usually tops the list. To start a conversation with you about his or her sexuality is, at the very least, uncomfortable. Knowing how you feel about homosexuality may provoke in your child a sense of exquisite vulnerability.

It is very important that you remember that your child's identity is vastly larger than the aspect of his or her personality that is sexual orientation. If s/he has been hiding that s/he is gay, s/he may have lost that perspective. Shame grows in silence and it grows out of proportion, trumping all positive and uplifting thoughts. When a closeted gay child is well liked by his or her peers, s/he may privately think, *If they knew I was gay, they wouldn't like me*. When s/he is selected for an honor, s/he may think, *If they knew I was gay, there is no way they'd be giving me this award*. In this way, a child's self-esteem is slowly eroded and s/he experiences life and any accomplishments as a series of lies. For these reasons, it is important that your child come to grips with his or her sexual orientation by talking openly about his or her feelings, beliefs and values. Your child needs to discover that people will continue to want his or her friendship and that s/he can succeed, regardless of his or her sexual orientation.

If your child believes that s/he cannot suppress his or her homosexual feelings while also believing that life, as a homosexual, is untenable, s/he may be in danger of self-harm. Remember, your child has likely struggled with his or her sexual orientation for some time before telling you. S/he waited, perhaps hoping it was a phase. S/he ignored it, maybe hoping it would go away. Your child may have a great deal of unexpressed guilt and self-disgust, because s/he deems him or herself weak, sick or unclean. It is important that you not reinforce those feelings. Whether you believe that homosexuality is a behavior to control or a trait to suppress doesn't really matter at this moment. Right now, the emotional health and safety of your child ought to be the first priority.

Coming out is a vulnerable time; so much so that some gay children consider suicide.[2] You must help your child recognize that sexual orientation is only one aspect of self and does not define him or her any more than any other singular quality. Any emotional or religious conflicts that your child or you might have about sexual orientation must be kept in the right context and in the right perspective. Challenging your child's sexual orientation or, worse, giving ultimatums, is a poor first response. Your first response needs to de-escalate the situation emotionally. It should buoy self-esteem and reinforce your connection. It should keep your child talking. Don't let your beliefs stop you from listening. Most importantly, be sure you communicate that, whatever happens in regard to sexual orientation, you will never withdraw your love.

······························

Chapter 4

What Not to Say

Some things well-meaning folks say to and around LGBTQS are better left unsaid. In this chapter we will discuss several statements you or others may feel inclined to say or perhaps have already said to your gay child and how they can be hurtful to your child.

- **"Why now? You weren't gay before!"**

  Many LGBTQs say they "always" knew that they were different. They can point to early memories of same-sex attraction and feelings that might not have been fully understood or voiced but were, nonetheless, undeniable. For others, self-awareness trickles into consciousness. It is a puzzle, the result of which is withheld from the puzzler until the final piece is pushed into place.

  There are many factors that influence when a gay person comes out to him or herself. Some of these factors are external, such as whether or not the individual's family, peers, school, church, etc., promote discussion of sexuality and are open to homosexuality. Other factors are internal, such as the individual's comfort with sexuality in general, the time of onset of sexual feelings and the intensity of the person's sexual feelings.

As with heterosexuals, some homosexuals are early bloomers while others are late bloomers. In the case of bisexuality,
there is a socially acceptable means of meeting relationship
needs that may reduce the urgency to act on or even acknowledge same-sex attractions.

- **"I don't agree with it."**

  This might be followed by back-stepping or a softening
  of position, such as stating that "it's between you and God."
  Signaling disapproval at the onset of the conversation pre-
  cludes the dialog from continuing productively. Refrain from
  offering your opinion about homosexuality before hearing
  what your child has to say. While this is good advice for most
  parent-child discussions, it is especially true when the child
  brings up something of a sensitive nature. By listening and
  not reacting, you will have a better chance of offering advice
  that accurately targets your child's needs. More importantly,
  listening demonstrates that you will not shut down and turn
  away.

- **"I don't care if you're gay; I love you anyway"** or
  "Don't worry. I still love you."

  When I came out, I heard these kinds of remarks a lot.
  It felt to me as if something was given and then taken away.
  Though seemingly supportive, this response implies that
  the gay person doesn't warrant love, but the friend or family member offers it "anyway" or "still." If your child is in the
  midst of a struggle with shame, s/he won't hear the love in
  your words. Your child will only hear hesitation and judgment. Instead of saying, "I love you anyway," stick with the
  tried and true, "I love you."

- **"Why did you feel you needed to tell me?"**

  Why do we talk about hopes, dreams and fears with
  those we love and those who love us? We do so because disclosure is an important aspect of intimacy and connection.
  If we are to be authentic and truly present in a relationship
  then it is necessary to disclose who we are and what matters
  to us. Your child told you the truth about who s/he really is

and s/he did so, perhaps, with some degree of fear about how you would react. Your child took this difficult step because, though hard to do, it was still harder for him or her to lie, conceal and keep distant from you. Your son or daughter couldn't bear to continue the farce. S/he couldn't keep wearing a mask, not with you. Your child needed to tell you that s/he was gay because s/he loves you. That's a very good reason and you can count it as evidence of the parent-child bond that you helped to create.

- **"Don't tell your father (grandparent, aunt, etc.). It'll kill him."**

   One doesn't injure, maim or destroy another person by disclosing that s/he is gay. Bigotry coupled with a lack of differentiation (the recognition of boundaries in familial relationships) might cause a person to overreact severely to another person's life decisions and that stress can lead to illness, but this is not the fault of the person disclosing his or her sexual identity. Love does not confer permission to control another's life. If you are afraid that your son or daughter's decision to come out will shock or deeply upset an emotionally fragile person in your family, do not ask your child to lie. Instead, try to prepare the individual to receive such information and support your child in delivering the news. Then help the shocked individual process the information. Consider sharing this book or seeing a professional counselor with him or her.

   Emotional fragility can be used as a form of manipulation. Threatening to commit suicide if someone does or does not do something is an extreme form of this. Not all emotionally fragile people are manipulative. Emotionally fragile people who are not controlling by nature are unlikely to overreact to information about a child's sexual orientation. If the individual is physically fragile, it is best to wait until s/he is out of medical crisis. When seriously sick, one's energy is best directed toward getting well. Even important conversations can usually wait. Your child has the right to lead a peaceful, open and happy life, regardless of whom it upsets.

- **"I don't want you to burn in hell."**

     People who say this may think they are saving a soul, when in fact they are wounding one. If you are considering telling your child that homosexuals go to hell, please reconsider. If your child is young and vulnerable, such a statement from you may kindle a shame that consumes him or her.

     As a practicing psychologist, I've heard and seen the effects of such a curse. In an attempt to avoid damnation, gays marry, remain lonely and celibate or attempt suicide. Sometimes they live dual lives, such as entering heterosexual marriages and engaging in same-sex affairs. Each of these "solutions" is terribly flawed. If you or your child holds a hell-fire view of homosexuality, I strongly suggest exposure to other religions that offer different spiritual perspectives. Many religions, even those which disagree with homosexuality, do not think being gay is a fast track to hell.

- **"That's so gay." "You're gay." "You fag." "You look like a fairy."**

     Sadly, the pejoratives "that's gay" and "you're gay" seem in vogue with adolescents today, though this seems at odds with the growing trend of acceptance of homosexuality, especially among young people. When gay children hear references to their sexual orientation used as insulting banter, it's disheartening. I suspect most teens who talk like this never give much thought as to what they are saying and how it might affect the gay adolescents among them. If you hear such language used in your church or school, demand that the adults in charge (teachers, principals, clergy) do something about it.

- **"Did somebody do this to you (e.g., were you seduced, sexually abused)?"**

     The scientific community has come to no clear agreement as to the causes of homosexuality. Most experts suspect that sexual orientation is determined by multiple causes, both nature and nurture. This is true for most complex aspects of personality. There is no evidence to suggest that early abuse causes homosexuality, regardless of the abuser's gender. No single factor, such as childhood sexual abuse, causes someone who is inclined toward heterosexuality to become gay.[1]

Sara's Story

Twenty-three-year-old Sara has been openly gay for several years. When she came home from college, she told her parents that she had been seeing a psychologist. She revealed to them that a boyfriend in high school raped her. She asked them, "Do you think I'm gay because I was raped?"

There was only one urgent matter here: the rape. Sara shouldered this pain alone for years. I encourage all parents to take a "no rush" approach in regard to any decision about sexual orientation. First, Sara's parents needed to communicate to their daughter that rape is never the fault of the victim and that she need not hide what happened to her. Second, the parents needed to support Sara's efforts to come to closure. Talking it through with them and with her psychologist may have been enough, but some women feel a need to take action. While it was likely too late to press charges, there might have been something she could do, such as writing a letter to the rapist. (Safety is a prime concern in any contact with an abuser. A professional counselor or psychologist knows how to assess the risk associated with confrontation.)

I've treated many people who suffered abuse and never has a heterosexual client asked if early sexual trauma caused him or her to be straight. Pathologizing homosexuality has led LGBTQs to pick through their pasts looking for a cause for their homosexuality. For those who've been sexually abused, there can be a strong temptation to "blame" their sexual orientation on the abuse.

While there is no sufficient body of evidence that can tell us if there is a relationship between sexual abuse and sexual orientation, for either men or women, logic goes against a one-to-one relationship such as described in Sara's case. About one in four women experience abuse at some point in their lives and the vast majority of perpetrators are male. If abuse causes homosexuality by driving women away from men, there should be many more homosexual women than are observed in the population.

However, people's experiences do play a role in shaping them. Bad sexual experiences can influence how a person feels about future sexual experiences. For instance, a woman with a history of sexual trauma will sometimes experience emotional distress or pain with intercourse, even within a loving and healthy relationship. Here, the impact of abuse on sexuality is clear. It is much murkier when one tries to infer causality between sexual abuse and sexual orientation. It's possible that sexual abuse, in some people, results in a willingness to explore same-sex relationships. I've worked with abused women whose bitterness toward men played roles in their curiosity and exploration of same-sex relationships. In these cases, abuse is a factor in sexual behavior, but sexual behavior is not always an indication of sexual orientation. People have sex for all kinds of reasons and not always because of genuine desire.

I asked Sara if she was satisfied emotionally and sexually in her relationships with women. When she answered yes, I was disinclined to think of these relationships as a reaction to her rape. I also inquired about her experiences with men and about her sexual fantasies and attractions. In my experience, people know to whom they're attracted, even if they are fearful of the objects of their attraction. If Sara were attracted to men (which would not discount her attraction to women), then she would be, at some level, aware of this attraction. I cautioned Sara against pathologizing relationships that bring her joy and I advised her to trust her feelings of attraction and follow where they lead.

···

- **"We don't have heterosexual pride day. Why do we have to have gay pride day?"**

  Every day is heterosexual pride day. The entitlements of heterosexuality are so ubiquitous they are seen as natural and go unappreciated. Proms celebrate a king and queen and not a king and king. Towel sets are printed "his" and "hers" not "hers" and "hers." Magazines depict attractive heterosexual couples. Movies about gay relationships are rarely seen in mainstream outlets and most LGBTQs will never see a gay couple reflected in a magazine in the dentist's waiting room. In some work settings, acknowledgement of a same-sex partner could endanger promotion. In most towns and cities, heterosexual couples walk the streets arm in arm without fear while it is an act of pure courage for a gay couple to hold hands. Heterosexual relationships are exalted every day, everywhere. When the same is true for gay relationships, there will be no need for a gay pride day or parade.

- **"It was just a joke. Nobody meant anything by it."**

  Not every LGBTQ handles gay "jokes" in the same manner. Some people choose to ignore them. For others, the context might determine whether they confront the jokers or let them pass unchallenged. I suspect that the stage of the gay individual's identity development as well as his or her personality and temperament play a role in how the person responds. For instance, an LGBTQ individual in the Identity Pride stage may be more likely to express anger than one in Identity Comparison who might treat the joke as a non-issue or even laugh at it. (Stages of sexual identity development are discussed in chapter 17.)

When gays react negatively to gay jokes, it may be difficult for heterosexuals to empathize. LGBTQs who confront anti-gay comments can be seen as overreacting. By virtue of their readiness to interrupt a pleasant conversation with complaints of gay bashing, they may be seen as self-indulgent.

Gay jokes register differently with LGBTQs than with heterosexuals. In general, heterosexuals are more likely to make allowances, such as assuming that a joke was made without conscious intent to harm, which may be true. They see the comment in the context of their whole impression of the joke maker, forgiving, perhaps, this one sour note in an otherwise pleasant song. Conversely, LGBTQs tend to hear a gay joke if it's whispered in a crowded room. When they hear one, they are less likely to care about intent. They feel personally put down, which is essentially accurate.

This difference in perceptions and reactions is understandable. Heterosexuals do not experience ridicule about their sexual orientation and so they are naturally not defensive on the subject. There is no wound and, therefore, no need to guard that wound. There is no pain and, therefore, no need to remain vigilant so as to preempt the next blow. Because they are not fighting a war against discrimination, heterosexuals are not likely to understand how a small act of degradation can feel like lost ground.

As a parent, it is important for you to know that gay jokes hurt people. They push closeted gays further into dark corners and add to the already heavy burden for those who struggle with self-acceptance. I think of gay jokes as the proverbial straws dumped on the camel's back. When I hear one, I fear that for someone in the room it will prove to be the last straw.

There is no easy way to close the rift in perception between sexual minorities and heterosexuals. I look forward to the day when mockery of LGBTQs is viewed as socially repugnant. Until that day comes, there are always bridges that can allow passage from one world view to another. Stand up for your child by interrupting gay jokes that occur in your presence. Listen to your child's insights and perceptions. By valuing his or her experience, you build the bridge that maintains your connection.

....

Chapter 5

What to Say

Maybe you don't want to say the wrong thing, but you aren't sure what to say. In my opinion, the most important words you can say to your gay child are: "I love you." This is the fastest way to allay any fear of rejection. The second most important thing you can say is: "I'm proud of you." This dismisses any assumption of parental disappointment. The third most important thing to say is: "I'm glad you told me." This conveys that you are not going to crumble and that you can handle this news.

If you are baffled or unglued by your child's disclosure of his or her sexual orientation, I suggest that you refrain, at least initially, from sharing those feelings. Instead, focus on your child's feelings. Ask, "Was it hard for you tell me?" "How long have you been struggling with telling me?" "What do you need from me?" If your child looks sad, ask about the sadness. If your son or daughter looks angry, ask what s/he is angry about. There are many ways to feel about coming out, including relief and happiness. Try not to make any assumptions about how your child feels about being gay. Staying focused on your child allows you to gather more information from him or her while collecting your own feelings.

When your child is more at ease with his or her sexuality and decision to come out to you, you can admit that you're confused or scared as long as you own your feelings. Owning your feelings is acknowledging that how you feel may not be how everybody feels or how your child feels. Your child probably already knows if you have a negative view of homosexuality, so don't be afraid to admit that you were taught to think of homosexuality as a sin (or whatever you were taught) and that you feel unsettled by the news that s/he is gay. Follow this with more reassurance that you are not going anywhere. You might try: "You're going to have to teach me about this. I need to learn more about homosexuality."

Don't rush in with advice. This is probably new terrain for you. When faced with new terrain, it's a good idea to step back and observe before forging ahead. You can look on the Web site of Parents, Family and Friends of Lesbians and Gays (PFLAG) to see if they have a local chapter near you. Through PFLAG, you can meet other parents who are making the adjustment to having a gay child. You can also meet parents who are completely at ease with their children's sexual orientations. It's a good idea to find varied and reliable sources to read as well. If your child offers you something specific to read, read it. S/he needs to know that you want to understand things from his or her perspective. Your child will appreciate that you're willing and want to take this journey together.

The sense of touch can convey messages that words cannot. Don't wait for your child to reach out to you; embrace him or her first. Internalized homophobia or fear that you will respond in a homophobic manner may stop your child from reaching out for physical comfort. Your child may be afraid that you will reject his or her affection. I think it is very important for parents to hug, hold and kiss their children at some point during the coming out discussion. Touch communicates so many things. It reinforces loving words. It demonstrates that you are not disgusted or ashamed and that you don't see your child as an outcast.

Spend "normal" time together. If you and your child talk on the phone regularly, continue to do so. If you live far away, make an effort to visit. Plan activities that you can do together that you both enjoy. Spending time with your child is a reassurance of your commitment. When a person first comes out, being gay subsumes all other aspects of identity. It can seem as if every action, every moment, is a gay action, a gay moment. Eventually, sexual orientation will become integrated with all other aspects of personality. Until then, it is a swollen and tender part of the psyche. Taking part in ordinary activities together will remind both of you that, on a day-to-day basis, little has changed.

Do what you can to engender trust and transparency throughout your son's or daughter's coming out process. It is important to check in periodically by asking about how things are going with your child's peers. Be watchful of peer acceptance and rejection. If your child appears depressed or if someone important has responded in a cruel or rejecting way, be alert for signs of self-harm or suicidal thinking. If you believe your son or daughter has suicidal thoughts or if s/he withdraws, begins or increases alcohol or drug use or engages in high risk activities that have the potential to be self-destructive, don't hesitate to confront him or her. Asking a child about thoughts of self-injury does not put the idea into his or her head nor does it increase the risk of suicide. When in doubt about your child's safety, seek help from a mental health professional or from your child's primary care physician.

You don't have to say the right thing all the time to be a good parent, but you do have to be willing to apologize when you get it wrong and say something hurtful. You also must be able to talk about homosexuality until you and your child have settled on firm ground. Don't make the mistake of waiting for your child to resume a conversation that was cut short due to a misunderstanding. Don't let your child distance him or herself from you or s/he might decide that distance is the best way to handle the relationship. Initiate the conversation and keep it going until you get it right.

What does it mean to *get it right* with your gay child? This is discussed in more detail in the next chapter.

Chapter 6

Getting It Right When You Can't Agree

If every parent of a gay child believed that homosexuality was as natural and unremarkable as heterosexuality, parents would not be troubled by doubt and their children would enjoy their parents' enthusiastic support. However, some parents, even after reading this book and attending PFLAG meetings, will continue to believe that homosexuality is a sin or is unnatural. This is not ideal, but in some cases it is reality. You don't want to disappoint your child, but you don't want to lie about your beliefs either. You want to comfort your son or daughter, but you don't want to encourage a gay lifestyle.

I think there is another way to help your child feel good about him or herself for those parents who just can't accept homosexuality. The preservation of the parent-child relationship does not depend upon conforming to each other's beliefs. Many children adopt political affiliations, spiritual beliefs, childrearing practices, etc., in opposition to their parents. It's to be expected. Differences like these don't destroy relationships. People destroy relationships.

A difference of opinion about your child's sexual orientation is not the same as a difference of opinion about politics. Generally, people aren't discriminated against due to political affiliation, but your child may be discriminated against due to his or her sexual orientation. There is also the issue of identity. Politically, people usually identify as

Republican or Democrat, but it's a chosen identity. Regarding sexual orientation, identity takes on a much richer meaning. Your child will think of his or her sexual orientation the way s/he thinks of his or her arms and legs: It's just a part of him or her.

I think that you can disagree about homosexuality without doing irreparable damage to your son or daughter or to your relationship with your child, but you need to disagree respectfully, humbly and in a restrained manner.

Next, I offer tips about managing differences of opinion with your children. Some are unique to handling differences of opinion about homosexuality. If you take these to heart, I think you can still have a good relationship with your gay child even if you struggle with accepting homosexuality.

- **Accept your child. Give up any desire to change him or her.**
  People can't change because you want them to change, even if they think you're right and they're wrong, even if they love you and want desperately to make you happy, even if you threaten them, bribe them, cajole them or manipulate them. Change doesn't work that way. People can alter their behavior to please, placate or avoid punishment and they can hide or bury parts of themselves for great lengths of time, but that isn't the same as changing. Pretending to be someone different is painful and consumes a great deal of energy. There is only one reason that people change and that is because they want to change.

  People can change, such as the alcoholic who gives up drinking or the criminal who forfeits his old ways for the straight and narrow, but lasting, transformative change occurs under certain conditions: The change must be desired, it must be separate from any external forces and it must be possible. Gays can alter behavior, but they cannot change to whom they are attracted; it is not possible.

  My mother says, "You can't change anyone and it's cruel to try." This statement is particularly true when a parent asks a child to stop being gay. The greater the love between two people, the crueler it is to demand change, because though love cannot produce change, it can compel a strong person to suffer beyond measure, to bend until broken. You don't have to agree with your child's sexual or gender orientation to accept him or her. You just have to recognize and respect that you can't and shouldn't try to alter this about your child.

• **Don't give uninvited advice.**

An adolescent or young adult needs to arrive at his or her identity without intrusion, especially intrusion from those s/he might feel obligated to please. You don't own your son or daughter nor are you responsible for his or her choices. For successful maturation, your child needs the freedom to choose his or her own values and find his or her own way.

Successful parent-adult child relationships depend on the ability of parents to transition from teaching and controlling their children to respecting and honoring their choices. This transition should begin early and pick up in adolescence. The best indicator that parents have completed the transition is whether they give advice without being asked or only when solicited.

• **Take a firm stand against discrimination and hate.**

You can disagree about homosexuality, but you can't support discrimination against gays and still hope to find common ground with your gay child. All forms of discrimination, legal and illegal, have a negative effect on health and well-being. If your gay child discovers, directly or indirectly, that you have colluded in his or her oppression, s/he will be deeply wounded and your relationship will be scarred.

If you are affiliated with people, organizations or movements that make it their mission to single out gays for attack, you will have to make some choices. You will have to rethink your loyalties. For instance, if your preacher is vehemently anti-gay, find another church. If you support a political candidate who has an anti-gay agenda, look for alternative candidates. I suggest you go a step further. Talk to the anti-gay preacher or candidate and tell the person that you have a gay child. Educate the person about discrimination. Let the person know that s/he will lose your support if that person doesn't allow your son or daughter to live in peace.

If you're a Republican, I don't think you have to become a Democrat to maintain a close relationship with your gay child. You should, however, talk with your son or daughter about political issues.

For example, Matthew Shepard, a young gay man, was lured out of a bar in Wyoming by two men claiming they were gay, kidnapped, pistol whipped, tied to a fence and left to die. During hearings about a hate crimes bill named after Shepard, Virginia Foxx, a Republican congresswoman, commented that "The hate crimes bill that's called the Matthew Shepard bill is named after a very unfortunate incident where a young man was killed in the commitment of a robbery. It wasn't because he was gay...it's really a hoax that continues to be used as an excuse for passing these bills."[1] In this case, you might say to your gay son or daughter: "I read the other day that a state representative said the slaying of Matthew Shepard was a hoax used to pass hate crime legislation. She's horribly wrong. I know we don't see eye to eye on everything, but I hope you know that this sort of behavior by a representative of my party really upsets me. I'm going to write her and my congressmen and let them know how I feel about it."

Much is accomplished by such a statement: This parent has taken an interest in his or her party's activities related to the issue of homosexuality, s/he has acknowledged a party member's error and s/he is making an effort to hold the party accountable to correct the error. That should win your child's admiration.

I encourage parents who are Republican to look into the Log Cabin Republican organization (www.logcabin.org). This group hopes to make the Republican platform gay-friendly. Perhaps there is something in their message that will appeal to you.

• **Get to know your child's LGBTQ friends and partner.**
Disagreeing about homosexuality is a poor excuse for excluding your child's partner from an event or failing to get to know your child's LGBTQ friends. Such actions are inhospitable and controlling. Mature relationships require a level of

emotional restraint. People need to be able to tolerate differences, even big ones, between family members.

Tolerance is making room for someone (or someone's beliefs) when you don't agree. Tolerance is motivated by humility and recognition that others' needs and priorities should sometimes supersede your own. It can be motivated by a strong belief in personal freedoms or by general good-heartedness that allows for some level of self-sacrifice to ease another's burden. A person might tolerate another person's music on a shared road trip or a guest's habit of leaving the bed unmade. These small tolerances avoid "making a mountain out of molehill." It's a bigger thing to tolerate homosexuality when you don't agree with it, but it is the least common denominator to maintaining a healthy relationship with you child. I hope that, regardless of your feelings about homosexuality, you see the value in being gracious, tolerant and engaging with LGBTQs, especially those LGBTQs who play important roles in your child's life.

Chapter 7

Parental Adjustments

LGBs have lower levels of parental attachment and higher levels of parental detachment when compared with heterosexuals.[1] This finding is disturbing in light of the power and importance of the parent-child relationship, especially to LGBTQs during the coming out process.

LGB children who view their parents as accepting of their sexual identities are less likely to resort to self-destructive behaviors to cope with stress. More specifically, adolescents whose mothers reacted positively to their coming out are 35 percent less likely to use harmful substances compared with those who are not out to their parents or whose mothers or fathers do not react positively.[2] In one study of Latino and Caucasian LGB youths, those who reported high levels of family rejection compared to those who reported low levels of family rejection were 8.4 times more likely to attempt suicide, 3.4 times more likely to use illegal drugs and 3.4 times more likely to engage in unprotected sex.[3] Another study found that family acceptance served as a buffer against the negative emotional and behavioral effects of bullying and victimization.[4]

Your reaction to your child's coming out is undeniably important, but not all parents can muster a "perfect" first reaction. Fortunately, your first reaction doesn't have to be brilliant. Second, third and fourth reactions can be just as important as the first. You'll have time to get it right.

COPING PROCESSES

The best way to avoid overreacting to your child's sexual orientation is to get in touch with your feelings. With insight, you will be more likely to cope in an effective manner. With that end in mind, let's discuss what is known about parental adjustment to having a gay child. If you've been feeling lost and alone, hopefully you will begin to feel connected to the many other parents who have had similar experiences with their gay children.

GRIEF RESPONSE

Parental adjustment to a child's coming out has been compared to the grief response. Esteemed psychiatrist and author Elisabeth Kubler-Ross determined that people pass through five stages when coping with a loss: denial, anger, bargaining, sadness and acceptance. Though generally thought to progress in a linear fashion, there may be some back and forth and bouncing among stages. It is not uncommon for people to circle through the stages over and over as they deal with different aspects of the loss. For instance, a parent's first journey through grief might be sadness associated with the loss of the son's heterosexual identity and the entitlements associated with that identity. Later, the parent might grieve the loss of never gaining (through marriage) the daughter the parent always wanted. In this way, grief passes through many layers, one at a time.

FORMS OF DENIAL AND ACCEPTANCE

Author Ann Muller identified four types of parental reactions to a child's disclosure of being gay:[5]

- **Loving denial**, the most common reaction, is when a parent offers words of acceptance but conceals the child's sexual orientation from others, thus belying incomplete acceptance. Concealment may give the parent time to process this new information before sharing it with others. However, if the parent doesn't come around to mirroring the child's level of disclosure, the child may interpret the parent's concealment as a sign of shame.

- **Resentful denial** is marked by a parent's physical or emotional withdrawal from the parent-child relationship. This can be particularly painful to a child who may already be struggling with feeling unacceptable or even untouchable.
- **Loving open** response is the ideal and involves both communication and behaviors that denote acceptance. Parents who respond in this manner maintain close connections with their children as they work through the adjustment to their children's sexual orientations.
- **Hostile recognition** is the most damaging to a child. This response usually includes demeaning and stereotypic accusations and the parent throwing the child out of the house. Reactions like this can result in permanent estrangement. Don't force your child to leave home. Though parents who kick their children out often take them back in, it may prove to be too late: "Holding onto the belief that parents will eventually come around is not always within [gay children's] developmental grasp, leaving these youngsters at high risk for depression, suicide, and running away."[6] If your first response to your child's sexual orientation was rejection, I predict that you are about to shift to acceptance. Your willingness to read this book is a good first step. Apologizing would be a great second step.

························

Jeff's Story

Jeff told his mother that he is gay a few years ago. He didn't want to tell his father, because he knew his father would throw him out of the house. Jeff's mother thought this prudent. Her husband was always making nasty comments about "homos" and "faggots." When Jeff was sixteen, he began coming home late and then not coming home at all. Jeff's mom asked him about his absences and he told her that he was in love. He explained to her that he and his boyfriend were going to drop out of high school and travel across the country together.

There is a litany of problems in Jeff's life that complicates his coming out to his father. His parents have an unhealthy relationship that models fear and disconnection. Because of his father's vitriol toward homosexuality, Jeff is exposed to a level of homophobia tantamount to emotional abuse. His mother's passivity has created an untenable situation for her son. In order to be true to his sexual orientation, Jeff feels he must escape from his home.

Jeff may have naively—or as a pretext to pacify his mother—described this plan as a trip, but in reality Jeff is running away. According to the National Gay and Lesbian Task Force, as many as 20 to 40 percent of homeless youths are gay, lesbian or bisexual.[7] While less research is available on transgender youths, the number is probably higher. LGBTQ runaways are sometimes referred to as "throwaways." If Jeff and his partner hit the streets, their chances are poor. Failing to complete his high school degree will create additional challenges. Runaways encounter many dangers and gay runaways fare worse than their straight peers. Jeff and his partner will be at risk for drug abuse, sexual exploitation and suicide.

I strongly advised Jeff's mom that she insist he stay and finish high school. In exchange, she should promise him that she will give him a safe and open home where he and his partner are welcomed. In doing so, she should assure her son that any marital problems that arise from this action are not his fault nor his problem. The fault and problem lies with his father. Jeff's mom should privately confront her husband about his homophobia and the way he expresses it. I suspect that homosexuality is not the only thing Jeff's father rants about. People who have anger management problems typically spew anger toward other groups or people.

Jeff is still a child and deserves a safe and supportive home environment. If Jeff's father cannot provide that home, his mother should consider living separately, at least until Jeff is mature enough to set out on his own. The safety of children, physically and emotionally, must take precedence over adult relationships, even marital ones. This is, in my opinion, the most basic parenting responsibility.

SOCIAL COPING METHODS

In one of the few studies that considered how a parent's social life and social support was affected by a child's coming out, Dr. Susan

Saltzburg, an associate professor in the College of Social Work at Ohio State University, interviewed parents who were in the acute stages of adjusting to their adolescents' coming out. She observed two dimensions of experience: one that leads to social withdrawal and isolation and another that leads to social realignment and connection.[8]

SOCIAL WITHDRAWAL THEMES

- **Creating Walls and Distance:** In this reaction, parents perceive having a gay child as a threat to their well-being and panic ensues. At the heart of this is fear of being rejected or treated harshly by those who hold a negative view of homosexuality. In response, parents isolate themselves. They refuse calls from friends, pull away from social contacts and may even avoid leaving the house.
- **Grieving Without Understanding**: Parents feel that discovering their child is gay is equivalent to losing that child to death. The grief is so intense that they may cry for days or weeks. Homosexuality looms so large that, for the parents, it envelops all other aspects of the child's personhood.
- **Too Stigmatizing to Talk About:** Admitting that they grew up in a time when sexual orientation was taboo, parents with this reaction are unable to bring themselves to talk about homosexuality. Conservative religious upbringings usually play a role in shaping this belief. The parents feel that the stigma of homosexuality falls not only on the child, but on them as well.
- **Fearing that Family Relationships Cannot Be Sustained**: These parents withdraw from one or more family members due to the assumption that the family member's deeply entrenched views preclude any chance of acceptance. Sometimes this can happen between spouses, resulting in a diminished spousal relationship.
- **Feeling Utterly Alone in Their Circumstances**: Having found no one who seems to understand the profundity of their experience, these parents doubt that anyone can. As a result, they isolate themselves, failing to lean on those who might be able to empathize.

- **Living the Secret**: As a means of preserving social acceptance, these parents make demands on their child to play down being gay. They also ask siblings and other family members to keep the secret. They withdraw, lie and obfuscate in an attempt to pass as a straight family. Much like closeted gays, closeted families feel the psychological drain, the lack of authenticity in external relationships and the shame of hiding.
- **Feeling Like an Outcast**: Feeling self-conscious and vulnerable to stigmatization, these parents align themselves at the social periphery. They see themselves as separated from the familiar flow of life and cut off from the support of mainstream parents.

All of the parents in Saltzburg's study yearned to talk to someone who had personally experienced what they were going through. Here are some ways that parents reach out to connect with others.

SOCIAL REALIGNMENT AND CONNECTION THEMES

- **Discovering Information**: These parents seek information, whether through people, books or television programs. Parents who use this style of coping feel less alone and gain new insights about homosexuality.
- **Experiencing Mentorship from the Gay Community**: These parents seek LGB mentors. Mentors help normalize homosexuality and allow parents to see that their child can have a full and happy future. Ultimately, gay mentors can become extended family.
- **Finding a Community of Like-Parent Peers**: Parents who utilize this coping style seek other parents who have gay children. Finding someone to talk to who is at the same stage of adjustment helps parents feel less alone. Without worrying about feeling judged, they are able to talk freely about sadness and disappointment and, by talking, they are able to move through the process of adjusting.

You can probably identify with one or more of these adjustment themes and coping styles. If so, you have a sense of what helps and what doesn't help you move toward acceptance. Isolation and withdrawal do not help and neither does committing your family or child to a life of secrecy. I strongly advise that you remain uncompromising in protecting your child's right to be out and open at family and social functions. Failure to do so is colluding with the forces that seek to shame your child.

It may take courage, but you need to reach out and find support. If you anticipate a poor reaction from those in your current social circle, you may need to extend that circle. Some of the parents in Saltzburg's study approached people whom they thought might be gay in an attempt to connect with someone who could help them understand coming out and homosexuality. Others attended PFLAG meetings or met parents of gay children at their children's gay support groups. The best way to adjust to your child's homosexuality is to get to know LGBTQs.

SUCCESSFUL ADJUSTMENTS

Much of the research on parental adjustment has focused on negative reactions or failed to move beyond the initial period of adjustment. But families can grow closer when they rally in support of an adolescent who is coming out. By demonstrating loyalty and love, family members can deepen connections. Coming out can promote serious conversations about relationships, values and beliefs—conversations that have the potential to benefit everyone in the family. The disclosure of sexual orientation can trigger other family disclosures, even ones that may be unrelated to sexuality. Disclosure communicates trust and trust can spread in a family.

Jeff Beeler, University of Chicago neurobiologist, and Vicky DiProva, former director of the Lesbian Community Cancer Project of Chicago, studied not only parents, but also families that successfully reintegrated after a child's coming out. The research team found that a family's experience can mirror the gay child's experience.[9] For instance, families have "finding out stories" that they need to share with others. They immerse themselves in gay culture, sometimes becoming quite sophisticated on gay issues. They go through a similar process of deciding who to come out to and when to come out based on the same factors that drive these decisions for gays. They see and hear things with a new vigilance for homophobia. Sometimes they become advocates for change. They look back in time and "restory" gay family members' pasts. For example, a history of poor self-esteem might be understood in retrospect as a symptom of internalized homophobia. A boy's failure to find a girlfriend, previously attributed to being overly picky, is now correctly attributed to an absence of opposite-sex attraction.

Families that successfully adjust to a child's coming out are also willing to remodel themselves, incorporating new rituals and traditions that draw the gay member and his or her partner into the fold. Inherent in the description of these families is an unyielding optimism. These families accept that things are different from what they expected, but difference isn't equated with disappointment. Instead, life's surprises are embraced as opportunities for growth.

PART II
....
HOMOPHOBIA

....
Understanding Homophobia

Some people describe homophobia as a fear of homosexuals and anything associated with homosexuality. Others describe it as ignorance compounded by dislike, repulsion or hate. Taking both of these descriptions into account, homophobia is "a broad range of antigay tendencies including social avoidance, stereotypic beliefs, intolerance toward gay rights, [and] morality concerns."[1] Homophobia is even in the language we use when we talk about sexual orientation. Heterosexuals are "straight," implying that homosexuals are bent or broken.

There are consistent findings regarding the general population and homophobic attitudes. Men are more homophobic than women, especially toward gay men.[2] Those who attend weekly religious services are more homophobic than those who never participate in religious services.[3] Those who identify as Catholic and Conservative Protestant are more homophobic than non-affiliated, moderate or liberal Christians and non-Christians. Dr. Bernie Sue Newman, associate professor at the School of Social Work at the University of Pittsburgh, found similar results regarding religion, with Conservative Protestants harboring the most negative views of gays and Atheists, Agnostics and Jews the least negative.[4]

However, Dr. Erin Coale Swartz, in her doctorate dissertation presented at Indiana State University, found a great degree of variability regarding homophobic beliefs within certain faiths. Out of twenty-nine religions, the most variability in beliefs was among Conservative Protestants and Catholics.[5]

Contact with LGBs appears to decrease homophobic beliefs. Dr. Gregory Herek and Dr. John Capitanio, research psychologists at the Department of Psychology at the University of California, Davis, found that the more LGBs a heterosexual knows, the more positive are his or her beliefs about homosexuality.[6] Even watching television shows with likeable gay characters has been found to reduce homophobic beliefs.[7]

Internalized homophobia has a negative effect on mental health, increasing the risk for depression and anxiety, especially depression.[8] Being out and socially connected with other LGBs may not be enough to reduce the effects of internalized homophobia.[9] To feel better, gays have to disabuse themselves of homophobic beliefs.

By recognizing homophobic thoughts, we begin the process of weeding them out. If you see two men kissing in a movie, do you feel a twinge of discomfort? If you see a woman embracing her partner, do you turn away? When you purchased this book, did you feel self-conscious? Would you feel uneasy browsing in the gay section of a bookstore?

There are many reasons for homophobia. The most benign has to do with numbers. That which is most common in a population is "normal." What is less common is "abnormal." This simple fact puts people in minority populations at a disadvantage, because the machinery of everyday life is always set for "normal."

The Quakers published *Towards a Quaker View of Sex* in 1963, which said, "One should no more deplore homosexuality than left-handedness." Since then, many people have used this apt comparison to dispel negative notions about homosexuality. Just a few generations ago it was considered bad to be left-handed. There were even myths that associated left-handedness with thievery and the devil. It was difficult to be left-handed in that era. What came natural to some people was unacceptable and what was acceptable didn't come naturally. Teachers were told to force students who favored writing with their left hands to write with their right hands. No accommodations were offered: no lefty scissors, desks, baseball gloves or guitars. There were no lefty surgical instruments. Forced to use their non-dominant hands, some lefties experienced delays in acquiring a range of gross motor skills and they were automatically disqualified from certain occupational pursuits. What a waste of potential!

Eventually, people realized that attempts to convert left-handed people did more harm than good and researchers came to the conclusion that there was nothing fundamentally wrong with being left-handed. This understanding is so widely accepted now that we no longer think of accommodations for left-handers as a burden to society and no American educator would consider conversion.

Just as left-handers struggled to conform to right-handedness, your child probably struggles to fit into the heterosexual world. Many people don't consider adapting the culture to fit homosexuals. Why is this? In many cases, there's no meanness of intent, just a kind of ignorance.

Some heterosexuals are blind to the advantages of a system based on the assumption of heterosexuality. They don't see the accommodations made for them and they can't imagine what it would be like to function without those advantages. This is referred to as *heteronormative bias*.

As a result of heteronormative bias, sexual minorities have to work hard to get their points of view heard, understood and valued by the majority who may not see, understand or value their perspectives. While the need to educate people is crucial, the process is prickly. It takes a lot of courage to keep up the discussion when one is in pain and no one seems to notice.

As a parent, you can make a big difference. When your child tells you what it's like to be gay, no matter how excitable s/he may seem, listen calmly. When your son or daughter tells you that s/he sees homophobia everywhere, look for and see it. It's there. If you do this, your child won't have to feel alone in a world that may seem to be against him or her and his or her feelings and nature. Remind yourself and your son or daughter that what is common isn't always right for everyone and that, for your son or daughter, being gay may be the most natural thing.

Chapter 9

Dissecting Stereotypes

Homosexuality is a normal variant of sexual behavior, but in some locales and to some people, homosexuality is a sin, a sickness, a sign of weakness and a source of shame. This is a cold reality from which you cannot wholly shelter you child. However, if your son or daughter can learn to detect, disarm and disable stereotypes, s/he can successfully weather the storm.

It's very important that you not be afraid of language. Your son or daughter will undoubtedly hear some horrific stereotypic assaults. If fear or anger shuts him or her down, then bigotry wins by default and your child internalizes the shame. Harvey Milk, a former supervisor on the San Francisco Board of Supervisors who was the first openly gay man elected to public office, once stated, "If I turned around every time somebody called me a faggot, I'd be walking backward—and I don't want to walk backward."[1] Milk understood that by fearing words, we give them power over us. However, when people discuss insulting terms, they gain dominion over them. When people dissect hateful epithets, they disarm them.

Let's talk about some "names" considered derogatory when used by heterosexuals. The process of reclaiming is transforming some of these terms to neutral or even positive words, but this process begins internally, within the minority culture. Here are lists of derogatory names:

FOR LESBIANS:

- Muff diver
- Dyke
- Bull dyke
- Fem
- Queer

FOR GAY MEN:

- Fag/faggot
- Fudge packer
- Top/bottom
- Sissy
- Fruit
- Fairy
- Homo
- Queer

FOR BISEXUALS:

- AC/DC
- Switch-hitter
- Swinger

FOR TRANSGENDER INDIVIDUALS:

- Drag queen
- Queer

I recommend refraining from using these terms even if you hear them used in the gay community. The one possible exception is the term *queer*. As discussed earlier, this label is now being used more broadly as a positive term. Ask your son or daughter what s/he calls him or herself and also ask how your child wants you to describe his or her sexual orientation. Don't be surprised if your son or daughter calls him or herself queer but prefers you to address his or her orientation differently.

Derogatory terms often reflect underlying stereotypes. According to Richard D. Ashmore, professor of psychology at Rutgers University, and Frances K. Del Boca, social psychologist, senior research consultant and associate professor at the University of South Florida, a stereotype is "a set of beliefs about the personal attributes of a group of people."[2] Stereotypes about the majority culture are often positive, whereas stereotypes about minorities are often negative or limiting. Psychology professors Michael J. Brown and Dr. Jennifer L. Groscup, of Brooklyn College of the City University of New York and Scripps College respectively, found that homophobia was associated with negative but not positive stereotypes about gays and lesbians.[3] Here are some stereotypes of lesbians, gays, bisexuals and transgenders:

STEREOTYPES OF LESBIANS:

- Angry
- Man-haters
- Militant
- Vegetarian
- Don't wear makeup (unless a "fem")
- Dress like men
- Suffer from penis envy
- Never met the right man
- Never had good intercourse
- Inorgasmic
- Asexual or low sex drive
- Ugly
- Sexually abused as children

STEREOTYPES OF GAY MEN:

- Effeminate
- Dramatic
- Selfish/narcissistic
- Weak
- Overly sensitive to pain
- Pedophiles
- Whiners
- Fashion focused
- Materialistic
- Non-religious
- Too close to their mothers
- Afraid of female genitalia

- Obsessive
- Disinclined toward sports, mechanics
- Promiscuous
- Non-monogamous
- HIV/AIDS infected
- Sexually abused as children
- Attracted to young boys

STEREOTYPES OF BISEXUALS:

- Actually gay or lesbian
- Confused
- Very sexual
- Poor impulse control
- Promiscuous
- Non-monogamous
- HIV/AIDS infected
- Unfaithful
- Sexually abused as children
- Pass as straight

STEREOTYPES OF TRANSGENDER INDIVIDUALS:

- Confused
- Playing games with gender, not serious
- Histrionic
- Sexually abused as children

By examining the stereotypes of LGBTQs, several themes emerge. The first is that "gays don't have relationships; they only have sex." When you think of heterosexual relationships, do your thoughts jump immediately to sex or do other images come to mind, such as a couple holding hands, talking together, having dinner with their children or walking together down the church aisle? One way in which LGBTQ relationships are minimized is to depict them as only about sex and about sexual urges. With love removed, it is much easier to discount gay relationships and homosexual lifestyles.

A second theme is that of heterosexual framing. Gays are artificially placed into masculine or feminine roles. A lesbian is a "bull dyke" or "lipstick lesbian." A gay man is a "top" or a "bottom." In this way, the gay experience is forced into a heterosexual framework, but it does not fit. While it is true that there is a greater degree of gender nonconformity among LGBTQs than among heterosexuals, the stereotypes suggest that this difference is true for all gays and lesbians.[4] It also makes rigid assumptions about gender and sexual behavior.

The third theme is the tendency to stereotype LGBTQs as crazy, usually with the tendency toward being indecisive, overly dramatic and sexually suspect. The most dangerous accusation along these lines is the false belief that gay men are more likely to be pedophiles. Pedophiles are attracted to children and pedophilia is considered a unique and aberrant sexual orientation. The vast majority of pedophiles are men and, while it is not uncommon for pedophiles to target boys, most pedophiles target girls, who are more than three times as likely as boys to be victims of pedophilia.[5] We don't assume that heterosexual men are prone to be pedophiles even though most pedophiles victimize girls, so why to do we assume that homosexual men are prone to be pedophiles just because *some* pedophiles attack boys?

Pedophilia lies beyond the bounds of those inclined toward healthy adult-adult attachment. It is a bad idea to base suspicion of pedophilia on sexual orientation. Gay and straight relationships are essentially identical in nature. An adult is attracted to an adult. That physical attraction is often supplemented by commitment, emotional disclosure and mutual respect. The emotional and physical needs of both parties are seen as important. Pedophilia, on the other hand, is not a relationship. It is one person, an adult, dominating and abusing another, a child. Being homosexual does not, in any way, suggest that your child is at risk of becoming a sexual predator. People attracted to adults, regardless of sexual orientation, are not inclined to be attracted to or to hurt children.

Samantha's Story

Sixteen-year-old Samantha joined her school's Gay-Straight Alliance. She also plays basketball for the high school. With her short cropped hair, tattoos and adamant refusal to wear makeup, it's a foregone conclusion she's a lesbian. Her parents don't have a problem with her being gay, but they wish she would just tell them. They're thinking about asking her.

Sam sounds really cool, but nothing in her story suggests that she is gay. Stereotypes about gays draw many people to wrong conclusions. One such conclusion is to assume that every boy who likes knitting and every girl who plays basketball is gay by default. Many straight youths who are assumed to be gay suffer the same degree of gay-bashing as their homosexual counterparts. Joining the Gay-Straight Alliance is a sure sign of two things—that Sam has healthy self-esteem and a passion for justice.

I don't have qualms about Sam's parents asking her about her sexual orientation, but how they ask is important. Sometimes a question can be asked in such a way as to discourage a truthful answer. "You're not gay, are you?" ends a conversation rather than begins one.

Because of her involvement in the Gay-Straight Alliance, Samantha may have given the matter of sexual orientation more thought than most youths. On the other hand, she may be sick and tired of people assuming she is gay just because she likes basketball and cares about justice. I suggested that Sam's parents start any conversation about sexual orientation by applauding her activism. They should point out that her involvement with the Gay-Straight Alliance is a source of pride for them. They can share some of what they know about the struggles faced by LGBTQs and tell Sam that she may never know the powerful difference that her support may have made in the life of a gay peer. Her parents could also talk about their distress at the way some parents treat their gay children and state that it would make no difference to them whether their child was straight, gay or transgender. They might even ask if they, as parents, can do anything to join Sam in her efforts to support LGBTQs at her school. At this point, if Sam's parents ask, "By the way, do you know yet what your sexual orientation is: heterosexual, lesbian or bisexual?" she is unlikely to take offense.

· ·

Because heterosexuality is assumed to be the ideal, being gay or lesbian is presumed to be a failure in attaining heterosexuality. LGBTQs are not broken heterosexuals. They simply are not heterosexuals.

Chapter 10

....

Casual Cruelty

I am confident that your child can lead a wonderful life, but his or her life will not go untouched by the pain of discrimination. This is upsetting to hear, I know. My spouse and I joke about building a plastic bubble for our son so that he can roll about unaffected by all things harsh and cold, but as much as we want to protect him, we also want to see him grow and no one grows encased in a bubble. People grow when they are challenged and some of life's greatest lessons strain body and soul with their demands. Without a doubt, it is a hardship to suffer discrimination and yet, if one is open to it, there is much to be learned from oppression and overcoming it.

Discrimination is the prejudicial and unfavorable treatment of a minority population that limits that population's opportunities, potentials and freedoms. Laws can be discriminatory, e.g., protecting one group's rights while trampling another's, but much discrimination occurs outside of the law. Individuals can discriminate in hiring, firing and promoting. Groups can discriminate by excluding certain types of people from joining. Discrimination is often a covert operation, such as omitting a minority group from a history book or not mentioning the minority status of an historical figure.

The LGBTQ population still faces all of these types of discrimination, although the degree of discrimination varies dramatically depending on the country or even the state in which you live. What I would like to focus on is a kind of oppression that happens on an informal basis: the impact of being subjected to ongoing ridicule and the casual cruelty of words.

LGBTQs experience intentional verbal harassment that is directed at them and meant to hurt them. They are also at risk for verbal assaults that are not specifically directed at them but which hurt all the same. These nonspecific attacks come in two forms. The first is through public media. LGBTQs remain a target for many social conservatives and it is still socially acceptable to demean publicly those who live a gay lifestyle. The second involves the invisibility of gays and requires a bit more explanation.

Many people possess a natural inclination to censor themselves when the target of their bigotry is in the room, especially when they know they have to work with the person or otherwise engage with the person on a regular basis. The invisibility of gays combined with heterogeneity bias eliminates that restraint. Gays are in the room but not known as gay when a person tells a gay joke. Gays are in the office but not known as gay when someone derides an openly gay coworker for his sexual orientation. Gays are in church but not known as gay when the sermon stresses the perversion of homosexuality. In grocery stores, riding elevators or walking through parking lots, LGBTQs hear anti-gay slurs. These insults are made all the worse by their suddenness and by the implicit awkwardness of responding (if one chooses to respond) to something said in someone else's conversation.

Let me offer an example. A gay man, Tom, is at the home of Bart, his immediate boss at the company where they both work, attending a holiday party. Some guests are colleagues from work and some are personal friends of the hosting couple. Tom is engaged in an enjoyable conversation when one guest says to another, "Where do you get your hair cut? I can't find a good barber." When Rogan, the other guest, responds, his voice is effeminate and with a pronounced lisp, "I don't go to a barber. I go to Jeffrey. That's Jeff with a 'rey' at the end. He's a stylist and he does wonders with my hair." In his natural voice he adds, "I'll give you his number, but don't drop your wallet with him behind you." A few people laugh. One guest rolls his eyes and gives Rogan a stern look. Rogan adds, "Ah, lighten up! I didn't mean anything by it."

Tom has been standing next to Rogan the whole time. He is angry and would like to say why. Before Tom can speak, he has to do a series of mental calculations. He asks himself, *Who here knows my sexual orientation?* Tom has told his boss and many of his colleagues. He is fairly sure that another guest, Karl, the vice president of a division he hopes to join, has heard through the office gossip. He has heard that Karl is fairly conservative and Tom wonders if the VP has a negative view of homosexuality. Tom wonders if a confrontation with Rogan will impact his chances of getting the job he wants.

Eventually, Tom decides to say something. He begins to think about what to say and how to say it in a way that will be best received. By the time he opens his mouth to speak, the conversation has shifted to a lively debate over the best recipe for stuffed mushrooms. If he says something at this point he figures it will come off as socially awkward. It will change the tone and the depth of the conversation, forcing it to a more personal level. That will be appreciated by some and seen as indulgent and emotional by others. Tom wonders if he should pull Rogan aside and talk to him one-on-one. Exasperated, Tom moves to another side of the room and sits down on the couch. A football game is on television. Tom pretends to watch so he doesn't have to talk to anyone. He wonders, *Is being silent the right choice tonight, at this party?* Silence comes at a cost. It gnaws at his gut and soul.

Sometimes the decision of whether to stand up for oneself or let an insult pass is easy. Too often, it is complicated and painful. The burden of always having to decide how, when and whom to confront is one that most heterosexuals cannot relate to because they have no experiential context adequate for understanding. It's a burden that, I think, is somewhat distinctive of sexual minorities due to their invisibility. Additionally, there are ethnic/racial minorities whose appearances do not fit with stereotypic expectations, rendering them invisible. There are also many religious minorities whose identities are not readily apparent.

Is it possible to handle these situations with grace? Sometimes I engage people in a non-aggressive manner that causes them to think not about my anger but about their biases. A lot of the time, I blurt something out which silences the homophobes but does little to change their hearts and minds. And then there are many days when I don't feel like educating anyone about homophobia. I say nothing and feel angry and bitter later. Confronting homophobia is no small feat. It is a war with many, many battles.

Encourage your child to be aware of the anger and disappointment that can build and to recognize when s/he needs to step back. Not all homophobic remarks are unanticipated blows. Sometimes they can be anticipated and avoided. For instance, if your child is listening to the radio and a socially conservative candidate is being interviewed, your son or daughter doesn't have to listen. S/he can choose to turn the dial. There is a time to listen to negative rhetoric so that a response can be formulated, but there is also a time to tune it out. Gay individuals must do what they can to pace themselves regarding the challenge of homophobia. They must take the time and space needed to refuel, even though it means letting some negative remarks go unanswered. If I tried to respond to every negative message I've heard about gay people, I'd be completely burned out. What good would that do me or the cause of gay rights?

When I came out, I wish someone had given me this advice and I hope you will offer it to your child: There will be days when you remain silent and regret your silence. There will be days when you respond to disrespectful words with disrespect and later wish you had been the better person. There will be times when an ignorant thing is said and you pounce on it with such fury that you miss an opportunity to educate. There will be times when you desperately want to speak but emotion pours out of you, drowning every word you try to utter. Please remember that you did not cause these problems. Any perceived inadequacies related to your ability to explain or defend yourself are not a function of being less than the one who attacks you but, instead, a function of being asked to perform remarkably, over and over, in highly stressful situations. Be gentle with yourself. Don't expect to say the right thing at the right time every time you are presented with bias. This would be asking too much of yourself and it will distract you from your job, which is to be happy. In the end, there is no better response to homophobia than to resist being derailed by it. Refuse to limit yourself. Live your life shamelessly and passionately.

···

Chapter 11

When Homophobia Morphs into Hate

There are many frightening forms of homophobia. Some people want to hurt LGBTQs in any way they can. A "hate crime" is a bias-motivated crime. Social psychologists Dr. Gregory M. Herek, Dr. J. Roy Gillis and Dr. Jeanine C. Cogan compared the psychological impact of hate crimes committed against gays to similar, non-bias-driven crimes committed against gays. The hate crime victims showed higher levels of depressive symptoms, anxiety and symptoms of post-traumatic distress when compared to the routine crime victims.[1] When suffering is compounded by discrimination, the suffering is worse.

When a crime is deemed a hate crime, harsher judicial penalties apply than would normally apply for the same offense. The United States Congress passed the Hate Crime Statistic Act in 1990 and, as a result of this law, the FBI began collecting national data on hate crimes associated with race, religion, sexual orientation and ethnicity. After the Matthew Shepard and James Byrd, Jr. Hate Crimes Prevention Act was signed into law in 2009, the FBI began tracking hate crimes against transgender individuals as well. This information will be available in 2013 on the FBI Web site in the annual Uniform Crime Report.

There is much debate as to the accuracy of FBI hate crimes data. While all but a handful of states have enacted some form of hate crime legislation, some states do not include sexual orientation and very few include gender orientation among the list of targeted groups. If a state does not recognize bias-motivated crimes against LGBTQs as hate crimes, there is little motivation for victims to report. In fact, the FBI notes that their statistics are limited because some police jurisdictions fail to report hate crime data to the FBI or submit partial data. In addition, it is thought that many victims of hate crimes are weary of reporting violence against them due to fear of reprisal or fear of further victimization from law enforcement.

With these caveats considered, the FBI's *Hate Crime Statistics, 2010* indicates that about 19 percent (1,528 incidents) of all the reported hate crimes were motivated by sexual orientation bias. When considering this statistic, it is important to remember that only 3 to 10 percent of the population identifies as being LGB. Gay men were more often the target of hate crimes than lesbians or bisexuals.

WHY DOES SOMEONE COMMIT A HATE CRIME?

The fear that drives homophobia can be understood as a fear of the unknown. This is not unlike the fear one might have visiting a foreign country. When people first encounter a new culture, they are prone to exaggerate differences and to assume that their ways are the best ways. They soon learn that the similarities between cultures are greater than the differences. We discover that different doesn't mean inferior. Similarly, studies show that exposure to LGBTQ individuals dramatically reduces homophobia.

Unfortunately, some people aren't exposed to interaction with LGBTQs. In the absence of exposure and in the presence of anti-gay influences, ignorance can morph into hatred. A fear of being gay can give rise to a hate of homosexuals. In this case hate is self-hate manifested externally. The idea that people fixate on a particular "weakness" in others because they cannot tolerate that "weakness" in themselves has existed for centuries. It is the implication of Shakespeare's "The lady doth protest too much, methinks."

One classic study dramatically illustrates this truth. Conducting a study at the Psychology Department of the University of Georgia, researchers Henry Adams, Lester Wright and Bethany Lohr asked a group of men to complete a scale that assessed homophobia. They then showed the men homoerotic video while measuring biological signs of sexual arousal. The men who scored low in homophobia were not aroused by the video. The men who scored high in homophobia were sexually aroused.[2]

Psychoanalyst Sigmund Freud and his daughter Anna Freud called the unconscious externalizing of one's feelings *projection*. Projection is one of a number of defense mechanisms that humans rely on to reduce unbearable anxiety, like those caused by unacceptable urges. When a person experiences his homosexual desires as repulsive, he will try to resist them. If he fails in this, the psyche may try to defend against this "painful" truth by hiding it from the conscious mind. To ensure that those feelings stay buried, this individual will hate homosexuality in others. Anything short of vilifying homosexuality puts him at risk of rethinking or reconnecting with his own homosexual urges. In addition, he may feel some relief by attacking gays. The hate he feels toward himself is buried but unresolved. It is in need of release and finds a conduit for release in aggressive actions directed toward homosexuals.

It is important to recognize that projection is an unconscious process. There is no strategy involved and no psychological insight. Occasionally, the projecting individual may engage in secretive homosexual activity. If he does so, he is likely to minimize or rationalize this behavior. He might flirt with a homosexual man and then become enraged when approached by him. If confronted while engaged in homosexual activity, he will likely deny it. If denial is impossible, it will surely set off a psychological crisis.

Not everyone who attacks gays is a homosexual in denial. Hate can be taught and passed on through families and institutions. Take, for example, a child who grows up in a church vehemently opposed to homosexuality. Assume too that he is home schooled and that the only children he plays with go to that same church. His view of homosexuality will remain unchallenged and will seem to him the only truth.

Hatred can also arise from poor self-esteem.[3] Desperate for a sense of belonging and worth, insecure individuals attach themselves to hate groups. These groups promise to accept them and tell them they are special and better than others. Superiority justifies brutish behavior and controlling others seems proof of superiority.

It's important to remember that most people don't hate gays. Thanks to the media, organizations and TV shows that depict like-able and upstanding gays and to the LGBTQ community which has worked so hard to be seen and heard, most youths today have been exposed to positive gay role models. As a result, attitudes are shifting and homophobia is on the decline.

Chapter 12

....
Religion and Homophobia

The greatest injuries are incurred when we are wounded by those we trust in the places we feel most safe. It is in these circumstances that our souls are bared and undefended. As is true for many children, gay children put their trust in their religious leaders and find esteem in the warmth and acceptance of their religious communities. Sadly, that trust has too often been met by judgment and rejection, particularly in conservative, evangelical Christian churches. Literary critic and writer Bruce Bawer said in *The Advocate*, "Straight Americans need...an education of the heart and soul. They must understand—to begin with—how it can feel to spend years denying your own deepest truths, to sit silently through classes, meals, and church services while people you love toss off remarks that brutalize your soul."[1]

Active membership in conservative religions has been consistently associated with greater levels of homophobia and sexual prejudice.[2] This is disconcerting, because when people are homophobic, they are more likely to act in prejudicial, unfair ways toward homosexuals. Gays who belong to conservative churches internalize these negative attitudes. They are more likely to see their sexuality as a shortcoming, more likely to have low self-esteem and more likely to suffer psychological distress than gays who belong to moderate or liberal religions.[3] When gays are homophobic, they suffer from mental health problems.

Dr. Bernadette Barton, associate professor of sociology and women's studies at Morehead State University, conducted a qualitative study of LGBs who grew up in the Bible Belt. For purposes of the study, she defined the Bible Belt as the geographic region of the country with the greatest saturation of fundamentalist Christians, including all the Southern states, Texas, Oklahoma, Missouri and West Virginia. Detailed interviews with forty-six lesbians and gay men revealed what the author described as "psychological violence" from the pulpit. Study participants described growing up in churches that routinely blamed homosexuals for natural disasters, death, famine and disease and threatened gays with eternal damnation. Close to 50 percent of those interviewed begged for forgiveness, sometimes weekly, in front of their congregations for feelings they could not pray away. Over 75 percent reported suffering anxiety, fear, depression or suicidal thoughts. The majority of those interviewed described "spirit-crushing experiences of isolation, abuse, and self-loathing. The most damning of these include rejection by family and friends, social ostracism, and an internal psychological struggle over their same-sex attractions."[4]

Manny's Story

Manny, a Latino teenager, is gay, but he has not told his mother. One Sunday morning, Manny came down the stairs wearing a rainbow earring and a pink T-shirt. The T-shirt had a big equal sign on the back and the front read, "Equal Rights for Gays and Lesbians." Manny's mother suggested that he change for church, but Manny refused. After Mass, the priest approached Manny and said, "That shirt is inappropriate." Manny said nothing. The priest continued, "If you are coming to church to make a statement about homosexuality, you're coming for the wrong reason. Homosexuality is not acceptable and neither is advocating for it in my congregation. You're welcome back, but only without the shirt."

On the drive home Manny's mother said, "Okay Manny, you made your point. Are you satisfied?" While the car was stopped at a traffic light, Manny exited the car, slamming the door behind him.

There's a lot going on here. For any number of reasons, Manny has felt unable or unwilling to talk openly about being gay and Catholic. His T-shirt is a statement, but what exactly is Manny trying to say? Did he wear the shirt because he thought the church, priest or both needed to recognize that there were gay Catholics in the pews? Did he want to make people think? Was he enraged by something the priest said about gays? Is he unashamed of being gay, even in church? Is he trying to force his mother to say something about his being gay? There is more to this: Why does Manny attend church? Does he go out of respect for his mother, out of habit or because it feeds a spiritual need? Is Manny's ethnic identity tied to Catholicism? Does being Latino make it harder for him to come out? Is Manny struggling to integrate several disparate identities: religious, sexual and ethnic?

Gay teens who silence themselves in this way worry me. Without knowing what Manny is thinking, it's hard to tell how conflicted he feels and what he needs from others. Manny and his mother have become disengaged from each other. From a distance, there is little his mother can do to help. I advised her that they need to get closer and the first step is to win his trust. Manny's mother can do this by demonstrating a desire to understand his feelings without judgment. It will be important to give Manny the opportunity to talk, without censure, about what it means to be gay, Catholic and Latino. His mother needs to encourage him to use his voice rather than act rashly in order to deal with his feelings more effectively.

....

RELIGIOUS AND GAY LIFESTYLES CONFLICT

Research from Dr. R. Ruard Ganzevoort, Mark van der Laan and Erik Olsman, of Vrije Universiteit Amsterdam, reveals that LGBs who belong to evangelical churches suffer from identity conflicts. More specifically, they are unable to claim both their sexual and religious identities. To understand the magnitude of this conflict, one must understand that what's at stake is not only sense of self, but also a sense of belonging. For many people, church is family, a spiritual home. Other "sins" don't put people in peril of losing their spiritual homes; why does homosexuality? Dr. Ganzevoort attributes this to polarizing discourse that has left homosexuals on the outside of religion and made them "the other." The study goes on to describe four ways in which LGBs can negotiate this identity dilemma:[5]

- **Religious lifestyle**. This strategy entails rejecting homosexuality and embracing one's religion as well as its solutions for homosexual feelings. Any lapses into homosexual behavior are regarded as sinful and there is no acknowledgement of homosexuality as an element of identity.

- **Gay lifestyle**. This form of resolution usually results in a rejection of formal religion and full acceptance of gay identity. Individuals who adopt this style of conflict resolution cannot rectify the apparent hypocrisy of a loving spiritual community with their experience of rejection by that community. Leaving the religion of their childhood may result in a sense of spiritual loss.
- **Commuter approach**. In this mode, "people move from one identity to the other, belonging to both mutually exclusive groups in what can be seen as parallel worlds." Often, this person maintains completely separate social circles, one with church friends and another with gay friends, neither of which is aware of the other's existence.
- **Integration**. The individual integrates the conflicting world of his religion with his sexual identity. He is out to those in his church, even though the church refutes the validity of his gay lifestyle. Sometimes integrators will make the move to another church that exhibits greater openness toward homosexuality.

Each of these ways of managing identity conflict involves some level of sacrifice or loss. According to Dr. Ganzevoort, if one has the tenacity for it, the integrator style is likely the best way to maintain both religious and sexual identity.

Parents who belong to churches that condemn homosexuality should ask their child if s/he has given thought to the apparent conflict between their religion and his or her sexual orientation. What are her beliefs? What are his feelings? Does she see your religion as a source of support or a source of pain? Find out if there are spiritual leaders or groups within your religion that disagree with the anti-gay stance. It may help your child to know that s/he is not alone. Seek church leaders within your organization who have a more welcoming approach to gays. Many people find gay-friendly churches that are affiliated with religions that, in general, take an anti-gay stance. Support efforts that allow for spirituality without sacrificing integrity and that allow your child to remain whole and true to him or herself at all moments, in all settings and with all people. If your child values his or her spirituality, help him or her find a way to maintain a connection with God.

For those parents who are considering ultimatums, please stop and reconsider. Taking an aggressive stand against homosexuality may drive your child from religion, a loss that need not and should not happen. If religious belief is making it difficult for you to accept your son or daughter's homosexuality, you may find *What the Bible Really Says About Homosexuality* by Daniel A. Helminiak helpful. This author explores biblical verses where homosexuality is mentioned and offers a refreshing perspective on Christianity and homosexuality. It may also help to explore the positions of gay-friendly religions.

Parents and integrators seeking churches that are more accepting of homosexuality will find many options. Among the most progressive is the Episcopal Church. Episcopal bishops were given permission to bless same-sex unions in 2009. LGBTQs who are Jewish can find a spiritual home in the Jewish Reform and Jewish Reconstructionist movements. These alternatives to Orthodox Judaism support gay marriage. In Reform and Reconstructionist temples, gays and lesbians are part of the rabbinate and cantorate. Even the Conservative movement has opened the door to gay rabbis and now allows rabbis to bless gay marriages if in accordance with their spiritual beliefs. The Society of Friends or Quakers has no hierarchy as is found in most churches. As such, there are socially conservative Quaker meetings and socially liberal Quaker meetings. On the whole, there are many Quaker meetings around the world that welcome LGBTQs and support legal reform for equality. Some other churches known for their gay-friendly positions include: Unitarian Universalists, the United Church of Christ, the Presbyterian Church (United States), the Evangelical Lutheran Church in America (and in Canada) and the Alliance of Baptists. The Metropolitan Community Church was founded to serve LGBTQs and now has as many as forty thousand members. (For a more complete review of religions, including non-Christian ones, and their doctrines regarding homosexuality, visit The Pew Forum on Religion and Public Life, available online at Pewforum.org.)

Chapter 13

Bullying

Judy Shepard, an advocate for LGBT rights and the mother of Matthew Shepard, a young gay man who was tortured and murdered because of his sexual orientation, stated: "When you call someone a 'fag,' it identifies them with a group that in today's climate is open to harassment. So, by calling someone a 'fag,' you are giving yourself and the people around you the license to damage this individual either verbally or physically."[1]

What would you do if you found out that your child was being bullied at school? The first instinct for many parents is to run to their children's defense. The next instinct might be to blame the school administrators for letting it happen. Some parents might teach their children to fight back. No matter what action you take, you will probably feel a degree of helplessness. In this chapter, I provide information and practical advice that will help you combat the problem of school bullying.

Bullying is a massive problem, affecting millions of school children worldwide each year.[2] While any child is at risk of being bullied, those who identify as LGBTQ experience more school bullying than their heterosexual peers. A survey of over seven thousand American adolescents between the ages of fourteen and twenty-two found that those who identified as mostly heterosexual, gay, lesbian or bisexual were more likely to be bullied than those who identified as heterosexual. The study also reviewed bullying behaviors by LGBs. Gay boys were much less likely to report bullying others than were heterosexual boys. While no lesbians in the study reported bullying others, girls who identified as mostly heterosexual and bisexual were more likely to bully others than were heterosexual girls.[3]

There is some evidence to suggest that students in the process of questioning their sexual orientations are at greater risk of being bullied than those who identify as gay. One study of over seven thousand seventh and eighth graders from the Midwest found that students questioning their sexual orientations reported the most bullying, the most homophobic victimization, the most alcohol and marijuana abuse, the most feelings of depression and suicidality and were more often truant than either heterosexuals or LGB students.[4] More research is needed to understand the heightened risk associated with students questioning their sexual orientations. I theorize that perhaps children who clearly identify as gay benefit from the social support of their peer group. It may also be that identifying as gay suggests a certain level of maturity and confidence; having taken this step, gay children may present to peers as more assertive and therefore are less likely to be victimized.

Children, both gay and straight, who are perceived as gender nonconforming are also at risk for victimization.[5] Because adolescents conflate gender with sexual orientation, gender nonconforming children are typically harassed for being "gay," whether or not they are gay. The more gender nonconforming, the more likely a child will experience bullying at school.[6] Those children who identify as transgender are at greatest risk for being bullied.[7]

About two-thirds of all gender nonconforming adolescents report being verbally harassed and about one-third report being physically harassed at school.[8] In fact, most gender nonconforming children have their first experiences with physical victimization on school grounds.[9] Texting, online chat rooms and social networking sites have opened the door to a new kind of bullying: electronic or cyber-bullying.

The consequences of school bullying are significant. Bullied youths have more unexcused absences, drug use, depression and suicidal behaviors than their peers.[10] They tend to isolate themselves, withdraw from school activities and fail to thrive academically.[11] They also are at risk for somatic problems such as headaches and abdominal pain.[12] Adolescents who are chronic victims of bullying may be more at risk for psychotic symptoms later in life as well as post-traumatic stress disorder.[13] Cyberbullying results in many of the same psychosocial problems experienced by those bullied in school settings.[14] This may be due, in part, to the fact that adolescents who are bullied electronically are often bullied in the school setting as well.[15]

School bullying doesn't harm just the victims. Everyone in the school community suffers when a school becomes a battleground and everyone benefits when bullying is stopped. The study of Midwest seventh and eighth graders found that children who described their schools as being positive environments where homophobic teasing did not occur had the lowest levels of depression, suicidal feelings, alcohol and marijuana use and unexcused absences.[16]

If a school's administration has the political will to end bullying, it can. A meta-analysis of forty-four anti-bullying school programs showed that when anti-bullying programs are employed, they are effective: on average, these programs decreased bullying by 20 to 23 percent and victimization by 17 to 20 percent. The more intensive programs were more effective, as were programs that included parent meetings, firm disciplinary action and better playground supervision.[17]

The Centers for Disease Control (CDC) offers clear guidance for school administrators seeking to end school violence. The CDC recommends that schools encourage respect, prohibit bullying, create "safe spaces" where bullied youths can seek support from counselors, teachers and school staff, encourage gay-affirming student groups such as the Gay-Straight Alliance, utilize health education curricula and materials that are LGBTQ inclusive, train all school staff on how to facilitate mutual respect regardless of sexual or gender orientation and facilitate access to LGBTQ-friendly healthcare providers.[18] I have a few more recommendations to add to this list of suggested changes. Schools need to assess where bullying most often occurs and consider making changes to the physical environment of those settings. For instance, gender-neutral bathrooms may help reduce harassment of transgender students. Also, teachers and staff who create and develop school activities should be mindful of language and roles that may limit LGBTQ involvement.

••••••••••••••••••••••••••••••••
Joe's Story

Joe, who is biologically female, has a male gender orientation. He has been in several scuffles at school due to his transgender orientation, but his performance in school is very good and his outlook about the future is hopeful. He works part-time at a local ice cream place. The owner has taken Joe under his wing and recently promoted him to manager. One day the manager called Joe's parents and told them that he was worried about Joe. Apparently, Joe had started to use the boys' bathroom and some students had been pushing him around.

When Joe came home that night, his parents told him that they knew about Joe's using the boys' bathroom. Joe told his parents that he can handle any problems and not to worry. Joe's mother asked Joe if he could use the women's bathroom for one more year until he graduates high school. Joe replied, "Absolutely not!"

A few weeks later, the school principal called Joe's parents to tell them Joe had been frequently absent for the past month. Joe's parents told him that skipping school was not the answer and they scheduled a meeting with the principal the next day.

Joe is still a child and children need their parents to intervene in unsafe situations. Joe's attempts to handle the abuse didn't work; quietly dropping out of school is not a solution. Joe may resist his parents' interventions for fear that they will draw attention to him and make matters worse. I counseled Joe's parents that they need to assure him that they won't send him back to an unsafe situation. If they can't remedy the problem with the help of school administrators, they should not make him return to that school. But they should insist that he finish high school.

A caring, competent principal may be able to come up with some creative solutions. If the abuse is contained to the bathroom, the principal might try converting one of the bathrooms, preferably one near the watchful eye of staff, into a gender-neutral bathroom. If that's not possible, s/he might consider letting Joe use the staff bathroom for the remainder of the year. If there isn't a Gay-Straight Alliance at the high school, the principal should work with school leaders and teachers to create one. If Joe is being harassed, it's likely that other children are being harassed as well and that the school is not doing enough for LGBTQ students. Gay-Straight Alliance groups use positive peer pressure to discourage harassment and it works. Though Joe may not like it, the principal should also discipline school bullies quickly and unequivocally so that every child in the school understands that harassment will not be tolerated.

If Joe gives the school another try, his parents should keep a close eye on the situation and act swiftly if problems reoccur. Joe should not be asked to "stick out" the year if he feels unsafe. If the school's efforts don't work, his parents will need to consider alternative ways for him to complete schooling. He should not be blamed or made to feel inadequate. The school has failed him; he did not fail the school.

Home schooling may prove to be least disruptive, especially because Joe has a steady record of doing well academically. Joe's parents may want to consider community college programs that allow high school students to complete their requirements by taking college classes, thereby obtaining college credits as well. Some high schools now offer credit for engaging in work experiences off school grounds. Joe may also benefit from meeting with the school counselor or a therapist. The therapist could provide Joe with a place to vent and may also be able to provide practical advice for dealing with bullies.

If the principal does his job well, Joe will be more optimistic about asking for help the next time he needs it. Joe will never forget that his parents put in a great effort for his safety, for his education and to understand his gender orientation. Transgender youths shouldn't fall victim to the belief that their futures are constricted by their gender orientations. Joe's parents, by their unwavering support, make it clear that they see the possibilities and they expect Joe to see the possibilities too.

WHAT CAN PARENTS DO?

Victims of bullying are less likely to be assertive. If your child is a victim of bullying, I suggest you arrange for your child to attend sessions with a counselor who has a social skills focus. This type of counseling will help your child manage conflict more effectively and may help reduce the risk of being bullied.

When children are bullied, it increases the risk of suicide. That risk is further exacerbated by feelings of rejection at home and by family discordance.[19] If you and your spouse are having difficulties in your relationship, you can help your child by working them out. When you manage conflicts at home in a calm and respectful manner, you teach your child how to do the same. If you are a victim or a perpetrator of partner violence, get help. You child will feel defeated if both school and home are battlefields. If you or your spouse suffers from an untreated mental health disorder, like major depression, pursue treatment. Untreated depression depletes a person of energy. It also leaves a person with a sense of hopelessness and foreboding—feelings you don't want your child to adopt. It is important for children to know, especially bullied children, that their parents are there for them and home is a safe place. Take care of yourself so you are available to take care of your child.

What can you do as a parent to ensure that your child will not have to endure school bullying? Find out if your child's school has an anti-discrimination policy and if that policy includes LGBTQs. If it doesn't, become an advocate and demand that the administration create one. Ask school administrators what they are doing to educate children about sexual orientation and gender identity and to foster a positive school environment where all children are treated with respect and dignity. Every school should have a well-articulated and well-supported policy in place that teachers and staff can follow if they witness bullying or if they are informed of cyberbullying. Inquire how recently the school administration assessed bullying among students. What was the method(s) of the assessment (e.g., anonymous surveys)? What were the results of the assessment? Based on the results, do you, as a parent, think the administration is doing enough to put an end to bullying? If you get resistance from teachers or the principal, take your concern to the school board or to the superintendent of schools. Refer also to the resources in the appendix, many of which provide educational handouts and example letters for your use.

Some towns are more gay-friendly than others. Where my family lives, the stores have rainbow stickers on the windows. When a gay couple walks down the street holding hands, they attract no more attention than would a heterosexual couple. Movie posters, without censure, feature gay themes. *Between the Lines*, a gay newspaper, is delivered to breakfast joints and people read it without fear of reprisal while sipping coffee and munching on bagels. The bookstores have "gay interest" sections. There are even churches boasting signs that invite LGBTQs to be a part of their congregations. The local schools have posters in the hallways that make it clear that homophobia and bullying won't be tolerated.

I work in a town that is only an hour away from where I live, but my experience of that school system and community is much different. In fifteen years, I have never once seen a same-sex couple holding hands in public there. The Academy Award-winning movie *Brokeback Mountain*, which features a gay couple, did not play in local theaters. I have never seen a rainbow sticker posted at any public establishment.

I provide therapy for some LGBTQ adolescents. The children whom I counsel report that their schools are not gay-friendly. Once, with my client's permission, I contacted a school counselor to let her know that my client was experiencing difficulties at school because the teen was gay. The counselor revealed that she knew she was supposed to offer support to gay students, but she did not agree with homosexuality. I offered to come to the school at no charge and give a talk for staff and teachers about the experiences and needs of LGBTQ children. The counselor told me that she didn't think the principal would approve and she didn't take me up on my offer. In situations like this, I help the children I counsel manage their school environments by being selective when coming out and by making use of support systems outside of the school setting.

If a school is slow or uncommitted to standing up for its gay and transgender students, you might consider transferring your child to a new school or even moving to a more gay-friendly town. This may sound extreme, but so are the effects of bullying. Leaving a hostile situation is sometimes a wise decision. Being attacked because of one's sexual orientation is a form of abuse. Suffering abuse does not build character. While activism can change minds and improve environments, children should not be forced into the activist role, particularly not as a means of emotional and physical survival.

If a child is being abused at school and the abuse cannot be remedied with the help of supportive teachers and administrators, remove that child from the abusive setting. No child should have to endure bullies and abuse in order to get an education. If you cannot remove your child from an abusive school environment because it is not fiscally or otherwise feasible, then I advise you to become a vocal advocate who will not stop until the abuse ends.

There are a number of organizations and online sites that offer specific information about anti-bullying advocacy. Among them are Advocates for Youth, StopBullying.gov, the National PTA and the Gay, Lesbian and Straight Education Network (GLSEN). These groups can help you learn about activism. Ultimately, it is the school administration's job to create a safe and supportive learning environment for every child. It is your job to do what is within your power to hold the administration accountable.

....

Chapter 14

Can Sexual Orientation be Changed?

Before we ask if homosexuality can be changed, we need to ask if homosexuality *should* be changed. It is not uncommon for humans to try to alter nature. Sometimes we alter nature's work because it has left a person in pain or with a deficiency in functioning. If a child is born with a cleft lip, we repair it. If a child has an infection, we treat it with antibiotics. At other times, humans alter nature's work to chase after a cultural ideal, such as when girls starve themselves to look like models or when boys take steroids to look like muscle men. Why do some gay children want to change who they are? Are homosexuals ill or deficient in some way or is it because homosexuals fail to meet a cultural ideal?

If people were less afraid of innate tendencies toward homosexuality in the greater population, I think the answer to the "cause" of homosexuality would be obvious. A good portion of the population, at certain moments in the course of their lives, is capable of same-sex attraction. Biologist Alfred Kinsey explains the "cause" of homosexuality in this way:

....

The data indicate that the factors leading to homosexual behavior are (1) the basic physiologic capacity for every mammal to respond to any sufficient stimulus; (2) the accident which leads an individual into his or her first sexual experience with a person of

the same sex; (3) the conditioning effects of such experience; and
(4) the indirect but powerful conditioning which the opinions of
other persons and the social codes may have on an individual's
decision to accept or reject this type of sexual contact.[1]

. . . .

While not everyone agrees with Kinsey's assumption that anyone,
given the right circumstances, can develop same-sex attractions, there
is wide agreement that homosexuality is not the result of poor or mis-
guided nurturing:

> . . . .
>
> Children raised by gay or lesbian parents or couples, for in-
> stance, are no more likely to grow up to be homosexual than
> are children raised by heterosexual parents…There is evidence,
> in fact, that parents have very little influence on the outcome of
> their children's sexual-partner orientation. It is also not true that
> people become homosexuals because they were seduced by an
> older person of the same sex in their youth.[2]
>
> . . . .

Though a popular myth, lesbian sexual orientation is not associated with higher levels of childhood or adult sexual abuse. The rates
of childhood sexual abuse and adult sexual assault are similar for both
lesbians and heterosexual women.[3] While a higher rate of childhood
sexual abuse has been reported in adult men who later identified as
homosexual, one cannot conclude that sexual orientation is caused
by early sexual abuse. Researchers suggest that gay men may be more
candid in their self-reporting than heterosexual men, who may hide
past abuse, particularly if the abuse was perpetrated by another male.
The implication here is that homophobia in heterosexual men may
reduce the likelihood of reporting even unwanted, same-sex contact.[4]

The myth that sexual abuse is *the cause* of homosexuality is
so pervasive and so intractable that an in-depth discussion may
prove worthwhile. In a recent review, Dr. Elizabeth Saewyc, professor of nursing and adolescent medicine at the University of British
Columbia, Vancouver, offers this cogent argument:

...if sexual abuse was a causal factor in gay, lesbian, or bisexual orientation, the majority of sexual minority youths should report a history of sexual abuse, and the majority of sexually abused adolescents should identify as gay, lesbian, or bisexual. Neither is true; in seven different population-based surveys across North America, fewer than half of LGB-identified adolescents reported sexual abuse.[5]

There is growing interest in the role of biology in the development of homosexuality. Some researchers have explored excesses and deficiencies of particular hormones and others have examined genetic factors.[6] These efforts either have failed to produce positive findings or the positive findings could not be replicated in subsequent studies. While most researchers believe that homosexuality may involve certain genetic and biological factors, the likelihood of finding a "gay gene" or any single biological cause for homosexuality is extremely low.[7]

Why is there such interest in the cause(s) of homosexuality? Homosexuality is still seen by some as a sickness, like an infection. If a cause can be found, then a "cure" might be possible. Paradoxically, finding a cause could also be touted as proof of the immutability of sexual orientation. It has been established that people who believe in a biological basis for homosexuality are more accepting of homosexuals. Having a genetic attribution of homosexuality has been found as the strongest predictor of positive feelings toward gays and support of gay rights.[8] How can people be blamed or ridiculed for something over which they have no control?

But if a homosexual could change into a heterosexual, should he? The emphasis on identifying a biological cause for homosexuality seems to imply that biology excuses what would otherwise be inexcusable, unacceptable or, at the very least, not ideal.

LGBTQs don't need a reason to justify same-sex attraction. They should not have to prove that they can't change in order to reject change. Homosexuality is a natural variant of sexual behavior and a natural form of love. The fact that homosexual couplings do not produce offspring does not detract from this position. Many heterosexual unions produce no offspring as well. Nature/God allows for all kinds of diversity, the purposes of which are often a mystery.

Researchers will continue to look for the formula that produces homosexuality, but I see no reason to look for a cause when there is no need of a cure. I see no reason to ask the question, "Can sexual orientation be changed?" when change is unnecessary.

SEXUAL ORIENTATION CHANGE EFFORTS

Unfortunately, some LGBTQs believe the cultural lie that tells them that being gay is a mistake, an error, an imperfection, so they look for a way to change. In some cases, parents of gay children fall victim to the lie and force their children into therapy in the hope that therapy will "straighten" them out. Interventions aimed at altering sexual orientation have been referred to as Sexual Orientation Change Efforts (SOCE), conversion therapy and reorientation therapy.

Many efforts have been made to try to alter sexual orientation, including surgical interventions (spinal cord cauterizations, clitoridectomies, castration, ovary removal and lobotomies), medical interventions (steroid and hormone treatments), aversion therapies (electric shock, shaming, ingestion of nauseating liquids), behavioral interventions (beauty training for lesbians, sports programs for gay men), spiritual interventions (praying, repenting, focusing on God and doctrines and exorcism) and cognitive interventions (reframing same-sex attraction as unmet needs or some other form of neurosis).[9]

Have any of these "interventions" worked? As you might imagine, the literature on SOCE is confounded by problems with design, definitions and measurement. Does refraining from engaging in same-sex encounters count as sexual orientation change or does true change require the absence of same-sex attraction? Is a person considered successfully reoriented by virtue of self-report? Given the pressures, both internally and externally, that drive people into conversion therapy, is a more objective measure of change needed?

The American Psychological Association (APA) devoted a task force to answering these questions. After two years of reviewing data, the task force published this finding: "There is insufficient evidence that sexual orientation change efforts are efficacious for changing sexual orientation. Furthermore, there is some evidence that these efforts cause harm."[10] At the very least, SOCE encourage negative feelings about being a sexual minority. Harboring such feelings results in diminished self-esteem, demoralization, depression, increased use of alcohol and drugs and relationship instability.[11]

Despite all of this, the APA recognizes that some individuals may want to pursue sexual orientation change. The APA recommends that providers of such therapy be skilled in multicultural counseling, be without any prior assumptions of the final outcome and utilize a patient-centered approach. Because SOCE have been found to result in increased despair, guilt, shame, sexual dysfunction, confusion anxiety, depression and suicidality, therapists must not blame their clients for failing to change.[12]

Unfortunately, the APA's advice appears to have fallen on deaf ears. The National Association for Research and Treatment of Homosexuality (NARTH), the most well-known sexual conversion organization, continues to promote sexual orientation change without acknowledging the lack of scientific evidence to support SOCE, the psychological risks associated with SOCE or the psychological benefits associated with acceptance of homosexual orientation.

Until homosexuality is no longer seen as a dysfunction or disadvantage, there will be conversion efforts. As a psychologist, I discourage conversion therapy. In addition to the risks, I fear that a negative experience in therapy will lead to a distrust and even resentment of therapists and psychologists. On numerous occasions I have treated gay patients who have shared stories of being forced into reorientation therapy which did nothing but leave them feeling angry or humiliated. In some cases, those individuals avoided mental health treatment when it was needed out of fear of being misunderstood and further oppressed. If your child is unsure of or uncomfortable with his or her sexual orientation, seek professional assistance, but find a well-trained therapist. Choose a therapist who does not display a vested interest in whether your child ultimately identifies as gay or straight. Good therapy requires neutrality; the therapist should not favor homosexuality over heterosexuality and neither should the therapist be confounded by stereotypes or homophobia. Counseling services offered by agencies or individuals who explicitly state a preference for heterosexuality are, I believe, fundamentally flawed, because the outcome is determined before the client ever steps into the room.

PART III

THE PATH TO HEALTHY ADULTHOOD

....
Social-Emotional Development

The respected psychologist Erik Erikson identified eight stages in social-emotional development. Each stage represents a challenge that can be met with success or failure. Erikson suggests that development occurs in a relatively step-like pattern. In other words, if one gets stuck on a particular challenge, development is halted until that challenge is mastered. While there has been debate as to whether Erikson's stages progress in a linear fashion, most psychologists agree that his theory is helpful in understanding the maturation process.

Human development theory has quite a lot to do with your adjustment to your child's being gay. Your child's sexual identity development occurs in the greater context of his or her emotional and social development. While forming a healthy sexual identity occurs at stage five, the stages before and after are important as well. Stages one through four provide the necessary skills to master sexual identity development. Stages six through eight depend on successful integration of sexual identity. Let's discuss Erikson's stages and reflect on how being gay might impact development and vice versa.[1]

1. **Trust versus Mistrust (birth to eighteen months)**

    The first stage occurs in infancy. If a child is fed when hungry and clothed when cold, if his basic needs are routinely met, the child will learn to trust. If his basic needs are not met or are met inconsistently, he will learn to perceive the world as unpredictable and people as unreliable. It's simple but important.

2. **Autonomy versus Shame (eighteen months to about four years)**

During this stage, the child discovers that she is separate from others. She is an individual! Consequently, she can assert her will upon the environment and other people. Colloquially this stage is referred to as the "terrible twos" because these first assertions are without benefit of reason and purpose. I'm sure you can remember a time when your child cried inconsolably because you didn't let her watch television or because you cut her sandwich horizontally rather than diagonally.

Toward the latter part of this stage, children dress themselves and assist parents with household tasks. Parents must keep the child safe while allowing her to develop confidence. At this point in development, it's important for parents to withhold unnecessary criticism. When a child picks out clashing clothes, the parent offers praise and suppresses giggles. When a child pours detergent into the washer, spilling a good share of it onto the floor, the parent congratulates the effort while offering gentle coaching on pouring technique. If the parent is overly controlling or demeaning of the child's efforts, she will feel shame, but if the parent supports the child's attempts at independence, then she will acquire the confidence that forms the root of self-sufficiency.

3. **Initiative versus Guilt (four to about six years)**

During stage three, the child takes on increasingly complex physical, emotional and social tasks. He learns to zip his coat, compete in a race, share his toys and express his thoughts and feelings. At this stage, parents can see the beginnings of goal achievement and frustration. Parents nurture success by guiding a child to reasonable, safe goals. If parents support winnable adventures and teach the child to manage feelings of anger and frustration, he will learn to enjoy challenges and seek new adventures. If the child's efforts are snuffed out or demeaned or if the parent is overly controlling and steps in prematurely to help, then he will stop initiating. He will tend to withdraw, to follow others' leads and to be hesitant to take on new challenges.

4. **Industry versus Inferiority (six to twelve years)**

Stage four is the phase of development during which a child achieves self-efficacy or a sense of competence. At this time, the child's moral reasoning is beginning to blossom. Whereas before she was motivated by reward and punishment, she is now beginning to understand how her behavior affects others. She wants to be a good girl and please important adults. If encouraged, the child learns discipline—putting work before play—to achieve a desired goal. In this way, she learns the many gifts that come from perseverance. By exposing the child to a variety of activities and by giving her the freedom to gravitate toward those activities that best suit her, parents help the child discover her talents. These achievements help the child feel good about herself and enable her to develop long-lasting interests. Failure to provide stimulation and encouragement can result in poor self-esteem, disinterest and the sense that one is less competent than one's peers.

These four stages generally underpin the ones that follow. Maturation cannot, I believe, move forward without the child having first secured a hopeful view of others and the world, the will to engage in that world, the confidence to take on challenges and the discipline to work through difficulties. These skills and attitudes lay the groundwork for a productive and exciting future, one in which dreams for career and family are fulfilled.

5. **Identity versus Identity Diffusion (twelve to about twenty years)**

The teenage years are when the seeds for dreams of career and family are sewn. At stage five, the adolescent considers his future. What does he want to do for a living? Does he want to marry and have a family or does he envision a future touring the world or becoming a rabbi or clergy member? Having not yet developed a strong sense of self, he is exquisitely sensitive to how others view him. Having not yet solidified his identity, he is painfully vulnerable to others' assessments and judgments.

Children at this age experiment. They experiment with dress, posture, politics, religion, values, food, friends, interests, maybe with drugs and probably with sex. One month your child may commit to wearing only black and proclaim he's gone Goth and the next month sport a dress shirt and announce his decision to pursue a business degree. While alarming for parents, this period of experimentation is crucial, because it provides the necessary experience to make informed and committed choices about one's values and goals. The development of a healthy identity requires that parents respect the adolescent's autonomy, including the need for extended time with peers and the open expression of thoughts and values, especially thoughts and values with which the parents disagree. Differentiation is the development of a healthy boundary between parent and adolescent. Failure to differentiate from parents protracts adolescence and can delay identity development or cause identity confusion.

A child will have to know himself well to pick the right partner. How many times have you heard someone say that s/he married too young or the wrong person? I think what these folks are saying is that they either did not know themselves well enough to marry or were still changing in substantive ways that would have influenced their choices of life partner.

6. **Intimacy versus Isolation (twenty to forty years)**

To have a healthy, lasting relationship, she must have mastered the prerequisite developmental skills: the ability to compromise, to make sacrifices, to be in touch with her feelings and to be willing to express those feelings. Intimacy requires trust. Trust, learned from parents, can be defined as having faith in the fidelity of certain people, institutions or a spiritual entity. People are selective about whom they trust. Intimacy requires the individual to be comfortable with and accepting of her sexual identity.

7. **Generativity versus Self-Absorption (forty to sixty-five)**

If a child's needs were met and his challenges conquered, middle age brings altruistic yearnings. Mature adults are motivated by a desire to give their knowledge, talents, love, time, money, etc., to the next generation. This altruism is born of a deep appreciation for that which a person has received and of a deep love and fidelity toward family, community, country, humankind and even to all living things. People who achieve generativity find reward in activities like volunteering and mentoring. Joy is found not in fame or riches, but in giving to others.

8. **Ego Integrity versus Despair (sixty-five to death)**
   The last stage of life poses the question, "Did I lead a good and full life?" There are many underlying questions as well. Did I love fully and tenderly? Did I act with integrity? Did I stay faithful to my beliefs? Sometimes the questions are more concrete. Did I produce something of worth? Was I a devoted spouse and parent? Did I treat my parents well? Did I give enough of my talents to others? The answers to questions like these set the mood for the last years of life. Satisfaction with one's accomplishments produces joy and peace. On the other hand, if looking back raises feelings of anger, remorse and regret, then the last years of life will be dominated by bitterness and despair.

You're probably asking yourself, *Did my son or daughter pass through the early and later stages of development successfully?* This is a useful question. If you suspect that your child has struggled with the preadolescent stages of development, you may find that it will be more difficult for him or her to work through identity formation, the fifth stage. It takes emotional awareness and confidence to come to terms with being a sexual minority. If your son or daughter has problems with self-esteem or talking about his or her feelings, your child may benefit from the aid of a therapist who can help him or her address these deficits.

· ·

Matt's Story

Matt, a young adult, comes out to his father, Jack. Jack is very comfortable with his son's announcement that he is gay. In fact, he is relieved! For years he's suspected it and he worried that Matt wasn't confident enough to come out. Jack starts telling the extended family and makes arrangements for himself and Matt to attend a PFLAG meeting. He tells Matt he wants to get involved, maybe become a volunteer speaker. Matt knows he is lucky to have such an accepting father, but he finds himself getting irritated by his father's actions. When his father walks in with a book about gay history, Matt says, "Dad, chill out, will you? You're making me nervous." When Jack asks his son what he means, Matt replies, "I don't know. I don't even have a boyfriend or anything yet."

There are several possible reasons for Matt's irritation. Maybe Jack tends to overshadow Matt and his achievements. Matt might prefer to reveal his sexual orientation to extended family at his own chosen pace. Maybe Matt is a bit shy or introverted and is uncomfortable with the amount of disclosure that his dad is creating. Additionally, while Matt's father may be well along in accepting his son's sexual orientation, Matt may still be trying to work things out for himself. Jack needs to consider where Matt might be in regard to the stages of coming out. Because Matt is close to his father, Jack may be one of the first people Matt's told. Matt may also be struggling with internalized homophobia. He may not be ready to attend PFLAG meetings or to have his father tell other people about his sexual orientation. If he lacks confidence in regard to his sexuality, he may have difficulty managing the range of reactions that are to come his way.

....

THE IMPORTANCE OF SEXUAL IDENTITY

Thanks to greater visibility and acceptance of gays, LGBTQs are more likely to address sexual identity and sexual intimacy on schedule, i.e., during adolescence and young adulthood. That's a good thing, because sexual identity is an important aspect of identity and suppressing it hinders successful completion of subsequent stages of development. Even a brief delay can result in difficulties with committing to adult tasks like going to college, getting a job, dating and learning how to be a good partner. If your child is deeply conflicted about being gay, s/he won't connect physical intimacy with love. Your child won't be able to imagine a future in which love plays a central role. In an effort to suppress sexual urges, s/he may be more apt to turn to drugs and alcohol. Indulging in these urges spontaneously, superficially and in a context of shame may lead to engaging in unsafe sex. These things dull the pain and temporarily ease the burden of psychological conflict without actually resolving the conflict. In fact, they are self-destructive. If your child believes the untruth that it is impossible for him or her to come out and be happy, than s/he may be at risk for the ultimate act of self-destruction: suicide.

If the pressure or the desire to please others overtakes the desire for authenticity, your child will try very hard to be heterosexual. This often involves getting married. Without real sexual intimacy, these marriages flounder. Sometimes one or both partners pursue intimacy outside of the marriage. Sometimes the partners stay together, settling for a friendship in lieu of true love. Unions like these reflect a failure to resolve the sixth stage of development, intimacy versus isolation. In my opinion, it is better to face the truth and dissolve the marriage even when children are involved. Why? Because living in misery is bad for everybody, especially children, and most folks can suppress misery for only so long before it breaks out and bleeds into the family. In addition, the marriage is a lie. It cannot model marital love, nor can it model happiness. If, after separating, the individual partners find their ways to true love, the children will see what love affords and want nothing short of love for themselves. In the end, authenticity is always better than pretending, both for parents and for children.

Failure to solidify identity, which must include integration of sexual and gender orientation, limits successful resolution of advanced stages of development. There is no way to fake being straight without living a lie. In this situation, when one looks back over one's life and asks, "Did I live a full, good life?" the answer will likely be plagued by regret. A life lived without integrity and true intimacy is a terribly shallow life, replete with pain and often absent of joy. I know you care about your child and want your son or daughter to be happy. Encourage integrity, living honestly and openly; it is the only path to happiness.

The next chapter examines the process of sexual identity development. Think of it as a process (sexual identity development) within a process (social-emotional development). Why does it take a *process* to discovery sexual identity? Actually, for heterosexual people, it doesn't. Heterosexual identity is the default. A person is heterosexual until proven otherwise. Coming to terms with being homosexual requires overriding the default and doing so against societal pressures.

····································

Chapter 16

The Only Way Through Is Out

Ellen DeGeneres and her TV character came out of the closet in 1997. For the first time on a major television show, homosexuality had a face and mainstream America was looking at her. There were open homosexuals before DeGeneres, but, from my point of view, she was the right person, at the right point in time and with the right kind of exposure to change the relationship between gays and straights in America. Revolutions take time and effort. Over years, activists work to draw attention to a cause. The tension grows tighter and tighter. Then, one day, someone says something or does something—just one more act for the cause—and the spring is sprung. When DeGeneres came out, she lifted a veil of invisibility that hid and muffled gays for centuries. Though a parental warning began appearing before episodes of her TV show, it had little impact. Gays were out of the closet and they were staying out. In her commencement speech at Tulane University in 2009, DeGeneres stated, "For me, the most important thing in your life is to live your life with integrity and not to give in to peer pressure, to try to be something that you're not. To live your life as an honest and compassionate person. To contribute in some way."[1]

Why is coming out so important? Because when gays come out, they no longer have to lie, hide and evade to make it through the day.

They no longer have to silence their anger when derogatory comments are made about them. Coming out aligns the internal experience with the external experience—that's fundamental to living with integrity. Coming out as a homosexual is like finding one's way out of the darkness and into the light. Whatever dangers await, at least they are real dangers, faced head-on, and not imagined dangers from which one recoils.

Coming out when one is homosexual results in better health. Disclosure of sexual orientation has been associated with decreased mental health problems, such as less stress and fewer symptoms of depression and anxiety, higher self-esteem, increases in strength and courage and improved social skills.[2] Coming out is also better for couples. LGB couples who are out report greater relationship satisfaction than those who are in the closet.[3] University of Akron researchers Michelle Vaughan and Charles Waehler considered how minority stress might foster social-emotional development. A careful review of the data on coming out revealed gains in five domains: honesty/authenticity, personal/social identity, mental health/resilience, social/relational and advocacy/generativity. Vaughan describes these gains as "coming out growth."[4]

When compared to LGBs who come out, LGBs who conceal their sexual identities have faster HIV infection progression, increased distress that can lead to depression and suicide, fewer job promotions and more negative job attitudes.[5] There is evidence to suggest that being in the closet may negatively affect work performance on both cognitive and physical tasks.[6] Hiding one's true sexual orientation is agonizing and depletes mental and emotional resources.

It is difficult to conceal one's sexual orientation. If you are in a relationship with a partner, try this experiment. Try going for one month without saying anything to anyone about your partner. If you have a ring, take it off. If you have photos on your desk at work, remove them. If people ask you what you did over the weekend, say that you spent it alone or with a friend. Be prepared to lie, because you will find that you have to lie a lot. You will also have to silence yourself and withdraw from conversations about family in order to avoid lying. If you try this experiment, I think you will quickly come to understand why coming out is so important to mental health.

Barry's Story

Barry (fifty-seven years old) and Carla (forty-seven years old) have been married for twenty-three years. The couple has four children ranging from fourteen to twenty years old. One spring morning, Barry showed up unexpectedly at his parents' door. He was pale, so his mother took his hand and led him to a chair. He sat with his head in his hands and began to cry. Once his mother was sure that Barry was not having a medical crisis, she called to his father and they gathered at the kitchen table. His parents pleaded with Barry to tell them what had happened and after a long silence he said, "I'm leaving Carla. See, I've been having an affair with...Mom, Dad—I'm gay." Barry's parents looked at each other, then back to Barry. With a look of utter bafflement, his mother said, "How can this be? You and Carla have been together so long. You have four children together!"

Some gay people marry heterosexual mates, but they do so for the wrong reasons. Barry may have married Carla in an effort to blot out his sexual orientation or he may have been in such a state of denial that he didn't know, at a conscious level, that he was gay. How could someone block out something as substantial as sexual orientation? The human mind has an incredible capacity for denial. Denial is a healthy defense mechanism. If you were told that you had a terminal illness, denial would slow the absorption of this overwhelming news, thus making it more emotionally digestible. But denial becomes a problem when it blocks absorption of the bad news completely. If homosexuality is repugnant to Barry, he likely denied his homosexuality. If he remained stuck in that denial, he may have married and remained in that marriage for years. Without a doubt, intimacy would be lacking in the relationship. Barry probably withdrew from sexual contact or used fantasy to become aroused. His fantasies likely provoked shame and/or dissonance that added to emotional distance between himself and his wife.

The drive for intimacy is powerful. In Barry's case, it is powerful enough to break through his denial. Initially, Barry may have seen his affair as a way to relieve a need without changing his life. To accomplish this, he would have to minimize its importance and compartmentalize his need, separating sex from relationship. Sex then becomes dirty and lustful and the marriage becomes sexless. Eventually, love or shame makes this unnatural condition unbearable and the truth demands to be told.

Barry is in his fifties, but in some ways he is going through adolescence all over again. Despite his age, he is just now reconciling his sexual orientation with his values. He is beginning to integrate his sexuality with his identity. He is planning a new future for himself as a gay man. Because of his age, he has dealt with crises and hardships before and this is to his advantage. He is less likely than an adolescent to see the situation as a crisis without end. He does, however, have responsibilities that weigh on him. He must consider how his coming out will affect his wife and children.

In these situations, counseling is very valuable. Individual counseling can help Barry understand the coming out process and deal with feelings of guilt and shame. Couple's counseling can help Carla express her feelings and come to terms with the end of her marriage. Family therapy, which would likely follow after couple's counseling, can address the children's questions and concerns. This will be a difficult adjustment for some, if not all, of Barry's family, but once they adjust, they will, in my opinion, find that living the truth is better than living a lie.

....

WHEN TO COME OUT

There are a few caveats to the general truth that coming out is psychologically advantageous. If the gay individual is particularly inhibited and sensitive to social disapproval, the stressors associated with stigmatization may override the advantages of being out.[7] In addition, a hostile environment can be so burdensome to gays that it is simply not worth being out. This is probably why many LGBTQ youths and adults are often selective about disclosure of sexual orientation. In fact, most LGBTQs are not out to everyone in all settings.[8] While coming out has many health benefits, being selective about when and to whom one comes out may have benefits as well.

What determines the timing of coming out? Today, gays are disclosing their sexual orientations at earlier ages than they did a decade ago. Recent studies put the age of first disclosure at about sixteen or seventeen years of age,[9] but a bevy of factors influence when any particular child begins disclosing his or her sexual orientation.

Gay men and lesbians tend to come out earlier than bisexuals.[10] There are probably several reasons why bisexuals delay coming out.

One might be that bisexuals first establish a "heterosexual" identity; this is the safest and easiest route to satisfying relational needs.[11] Another possibility for the delay is a lack of support from the gay community.[12] Bisexuals are sometimes viewed by gay men and lesbians as "passing" as heterosexuals and therefore bypassing the prejudice homosexuals must endure.

Coming out opens the door to discrimination and victimization. Social psychologists Dr. Anthony Bogaert and Dr. Carolyn Hafer of Brock University explored whether an individual's perception of the risks associated with being gay impact the timing of coming out. The researchers' theories and expectations included:[13]

- Gays who believed in a "just world" would be more likely to come out earlier than gays who see the world as unfair.
- Having a sense of self-efficacy and personal control— believing that you have the ability to tackle what you set out to do—would be associated with coming out earlier.
- People who saw themselves as physically attractive would come out earlier. Among other benefits, being attractive is associated with greater social confidence and greater sexual assertion. Attractive people are treated more positively and punished less harshly.
- Gender nonconformity would play a role in coming out, but the researchers didn't know if it would speed it up or delay it.

Bogaert and Hafer had some interesting findings. Gay and bisexual men who believed in a just world came out earlier, but this was true only for more effeminate men, the subgroup of men most at risk for victimization. This finding has to be interpreted with caution. Does a belief in a just world buffer effeminate gay men from perceiving coming out as risky or do these men have more experience with an unjust world and so would not come out at all unless they had a strong belief in a just world? It's hard to say. Self-efficacy and personal control did not affect the timing of coming out. This may suggest that the factors over which one has no control, such as whether a school is gay-friendly, play a substantial role in the decision of whether to come out. As predicted, physical attractiveness was associated with coming out earlier. The world is easier on attractive people, even those of minority status, and apparently people sense this benefit at an early age.

WHO IS TOLD FIRST?

When adolescents come out, they generally tell their friends first. This may be because, in general, gay youths report getting the most support from friends with managing stressors specifically related to being a sexual minority.[14] Depending on a variety of factors, such as religious beliefs, teens then tell siblings or mothers. Fathers are often the last to know. Most research suggests that fathers react more negatively to a child's coming out than mothers, but a recent study found no difference between how fathers and mothers react, suggesting that fathers may be coming around.[15] Caucasians are more likely to come out to their parents than African Americans, Latinos and Asian/Pacific Islanders.[16] In these cultures there may be greater expectations placed on children to uphold tradition, maintain gender roles and protect family harmony. Among African American families, adolescents often tell extended family members, aunts, uncles and cousins before telling their parents.[17]

COMING OUT WHEN YOU'RE EXPONENTIALLY DIFFERENT

Some people have more than one minority affiliation. In fact, many people do. To be seen as different in more than one way is not necessarily a burden. For example, some minority religions are more accepting of homosexuality than majority religions. Barney Frank, who has been a respected member of the House of Representatives, once stated in an interview, "I'm used to being in a minority. Hey, I'm a left-handed gay Jew. I've never felt, automatically, a member of any majority."[18] When minority identities intersect, the results can be surprising.

The research on race and homophobia is difficult to interpret. Some researchers report that African Americans are more homophobic than Caucasians, with especially high levels of homophobia among male African American adolescents. A closer look at the research reveals the relationship between race and homophobia is modulated by other factors, such as age and religious affiliation.[19]

At one time, it was thought that double minorities (such as being both black and gay) suffered an internal conflict between identities. This doesn't appear to be the case. Most people of color are able to coalesce multiple identities without forestalling identity develop-ment.[20] Certainly, double minorities face more stressors just by virtue of being subjugated to multiple types of bigotry. In addition, racial minorities are more likely than Caucasians to be economically disad-vantaged, with all that goes with it, such as poorer schools and reduced access to good nutrition. With all that adversity, one might expect to find double minorities doing poorly when compared with Caucasian LGBTQs, but this is not always the case.

While LGB adolescents of color commit suicide at higher rates than their white counterparts, the lifetime prevalence (rate of occur-rence over the course of a lifetime) of mental health disorders in Latino and African American LGBs is similar to that of Caucasians.[21] It is speculated that experience coping with racism prepares racial minorities to deal with homophobia more effectively; they are more resilient than their white counterparts and this added resiliency miti-gates the effects of having a greater number of stressors.[22]

If your child is of a different race, ethnic group or religion than the majority of people in your country or city in multiple ways, it may help to explore each of these differences individually and in combina-tion. For example, Kia's biological parents are Korean and the child is adopted as an infant by an African American couple. As a young girl she is diagnosed with type 1 diabetes, which is well controlled with daily insulin injections. As she grows up she finds she is bisexual. In a number of ways she is different from the majority of her peers. Kia has an Asian appearance, but her ethnic identity is tied to her African American adoptive parents and African American neighborhood. If she takes an interest in her Korean heritage, she might think of her-self as having dual ethnicity. While her diabetes disorder is not a visi-ble difference, it may make her feel different. On a daily basis Kia must closely monitor her blood sugar and administer her injections. She has to be careful about what she eats and when she eats. What about her bisexuality? If she attends a gay-friendly school, being bisexual may prove to be just one more difference and not particularly burdensome. If she attends a school that bans LGBTQ activities and discourages any attempt to form groups such as Gay-Straight Alliance, then being openly bisexual may take a lot of courage and may interfere with her success at school.

It will be important for this girl's parents to ask their daughter about each of these differences without projecting their own thoughts

and feelings. As she progresses through the stages of social and emotional development, what draws her attention is likely to shift from
one aspect of self to another. Kia's parents must be careful to follow
their daughter's feelings and not let their worries become their daughter's worries.

Culture plays a role in values. While the distance between countries seems to be shrinking every day, there are some differences that
still hold largely true. For instance, children growing up in the United
States are taught to be future-focused, but children in China are
expected to focus more on the past, to value the wisdom, traditions
and accomplishments of their ancestors. While the United States
places a priority on individual choice, some cultures, like India's, place
greater emphasis on harmony and self-sacrifice. Within cultures, there
are subcultures that have their own unique world views. Divisions
between subcultures arise from any number of factors, such as region,
religion and ethnicity. People raised in cities, whether Calcutta or New
York, may find they have more in common with other city dwellers
than they do with people from the rural areas of their own countries.

Whether a culture values individualism over harmony and
whether a culture is future focused or past focused are just a few
examples of cultural differences, but they happen to be differences
that affect coming out. It will be more difficult for a child to come out
if his or her culture tells the child that s/he should honor the traditions of the past and put the needs of others before his or her own
needs. I am not passing judgment on any culture's value system. In
fact, I find much to revere in such values. I am saying that cultural
values impact coming out.

It is important for you, as a parent, to understand the freedoms
and restraints imposed by your culture. With this insight, you will better understand how coming out as LGBTQ is in line with cultural values
or out of line with them. When coming out is mostly discordant with
cultural values, it adds weight to an already heavy task. If your family needs to deal with diversity, have an open talk about cultural values with your son or daughter. You may find that your child's coming
out allows you to stretch beyond your world view by incorporating
perspectives from other cultures. On the other hand, you may discover
within the richness of your own culture that a way "out" is already
provided. For example, in the Native American culture, "two-spirit"
people are thought to be, innately, both male and female. They often

cross-dress and engage in bisexual relationships. They are not bound by gender expectations. Rather than being shunned by their tribes, they are honored and sometimes even thought of as having magical powers.

Remember, minority affiliation is not straightforward nor the same for any two individuals. Having an affiliation with multiple minority groups is worthy of reflection, but that reflection is most meaningful when it happens at an individual level. Who can guess how one aspect of difference will impact another in any particular family, in any particular environment, at any particular point in an individual's development? I believe that being exponentially different has the potential to be exponentially enlightening.

······································

Chapter 17

Stages of Coming Out

P eople typically use the term "coming out" to mean the disclosing of one's sexual identity as non-heterosexual, but actually, coming out is a process that begins with revealing to oneself that one is gay. Psychological theorist Vivienne Cass's six-stage model of homosexual identity development articulates the inner experience of gays. Cass's model was developed based on research on gay, lesbian and bisexual identity development and may not always be applicable to transgender youths. Here are Cass's stages along with brief, experiential descriptions and discussions.[1]

IDENTITY CONFUSION

The experience: At first, a person is aware of being different and of having feelings that she cannot name and that she feels she should not talk about. Eventually she recognizes that "differentness" as homosexual longings. The individual is confused, because no one told her that she might feel this way. She feels guilty and desperately hopes that these uninvited thoughts and feelings will pass with time.

Discussion: At this stage, denial can set in, resulting in a delay or a shutting down of sexual development. If an individual gets stuck in this phase, she may adopt an asexual veneer or simply try to act like a heterosexual. The former type of denial makes for a terribly sad, limiting and lonely life, while the latter type leads to flawed relationships. People often wonder how a man or woman can come out as gay after years of marriage; denial is the answer.

IDENTITY COMPARISON

The experience: At this stage, the person can no longer deny that he may be a homosexual. Since the individual sees his homosexuality through a homophobic lens, he experiences being gay as being somehow inferior, sinful, abnormal or perverted. His future appears doomed. Hopes of having a great career, of marrying, of having children are crushed. He is struck by the realization that all of life's wonders are entwined with heterosexuality—every joyous occasion, every ritual, every imagined triumph. He recoils in despair. Panic sets in. He doesn't know what to do.

Discussion: At this stage, self-worth is in great jeopardy and suicide is a risk. Support groups are an invaluable source of hope. They provide a new, positive lens through which to view homosexuality. They offer a path to work for equal rights. Support groups help those who are adjusting to a sexual minority status to see that life as a homosexual can be a life full of grace, triumph and joy.

IDENTITY TOLERANCE

The experience: The individual now questions the majority perspective on homosexuality. As she makes the mental shift from "I am not right" to "society is not right," she becomes more resilient against homophobia. She can now tolerate the idea of being gay. As she moves toward identifying as gay, lesbian or bisexual, she feels increasingly at odds with heteronormative expectations, that is, the cultural bias in favor of opposite-sex relationships and against same-sex relationships.

Discussion: People in this stage may seem distant, withdrawn, socially out of step or awkward. In a real sense, they know who they are not, but not who they are or who they will become. People know how to be heterosexual: how to carry oneself, what to wear, how to flirt, even what to talk about and say in the wide array of social contexts which life presents. Parents, relatives, teachers, friends, TV programs, movies and books offer a plethora of examples from which to choose.

But what does it mean to be gay? How are sexual feelings communicated? What does gay and sexy look like? How does one flirt? These are just a few of the tough questions that someone in this stage faces. If s/he appears awkward or distant, is it any surprise? It is a balancing act to move toward a new sense of self while staying vigilant within a social terrain that is strewn with mines. Imagine what it would be like to be attracted to a same-sex peer, to want to communicate that attraction, but to want to do so in a way that will go unnoticed by those who might ridicule you (including the object of your attraction). Again, contact with others in the gay community reduces isolation as well as offers practical guidance that can help someone coming out to regain his or her social footing.

IDENTITY ACCEPTANCE

The experience: At this stage, the person has completely accepted his LGB identity, an identity that he sees much differently and more positively than he did at the start of this process. He begins to come out to family and close friends. If he hasn't been sexually active already, he is likely to start and, since he can now envision a future, he may find himself looking for a lasting relationship. He feels a tremendous relief in knowing the days of fighting who he is have come to an end. As he embraces his homosexuality, he also takes on new struggles. Actions taken against gays are experienced as personal affronts. Indifference toward the suffering of gays is indifference toward his own mistreatment.

The discussion: This can be a time of great disappointment and grief or a time of overwhelming joy and relief. Much depends on how others respond to the LGBTQ's disclosure. A positive response can enhance self-esteem and hope. A negative response can generate fear and hopelessness. In some scenarios, youths are disowned by their parents. Parents play a very special role at this stage of coming out.

Your reaction matters a lot, perhaps more than anybody else's. If your child ever needed your support and love, now is the time.

In the life of every gay person there are several moments that hold special meaning. One of those is coming out to parents. Regardless of how that first talk went, it is important that you remain open to talking again. If your adult child tells you about his or her sexual orientation by telephone, get in your car or on a plane and go to him or her. Your child will be looking for clues as to how you feel about him or her now that you know the truth. A face-to-face conversation demonstrates that you are not going to withdraw your love and that you are not afraid to talk. An in-person visit also allows for hugs and kisses. Affection from you can counter internalized homophobia that may make your child feel dirty, perverted or in some way untouchable.

IDENTITY PRIDE

The experience: Acceptance transforms into pride. The gay individual now immerses herself in the LGBTQ community. There, she feels a unique sense of belonging. Only other LGBTQs can offer the satisfaction of being completely and utterly understood and accepted. There is a thrill and a pride in being oneself without fretting and without self-scrutiny. She spent years in a prison of social deprivation and self-denial and now she is free. There may be anger and even rage at the heterosexual world that withholds legal rights and fails to acknowledge the pain and isolation that the individual experienced growing up. She wants people to get it. She wants them to care.

The discussion: It is important for a person in this stage to be free to explore what it means to be gay. If this comes during young adulthood, parents might see some radical changes. Most teens experiment with identity by exploring different looks, e.g., tattoos, earring plugs, piercings, spiked hair, etc. All this can be very unnerving for parents who must struggle with where to set boundaries.

Gay children may experiment with finding a look that incorporates signs of gay identity. During this stage of identity development, they may surround themselves with positive images: rainbows, equal signs, triangles. They also may take on a more stereotypic look as they experiment with ways of presenting themselves. Give your child room. In order to grow up, your child must "differentiate" from you;

that is, s/he must push off and become independent. If you make too big a fuss over something distasteful to you but not dangerous to your child, s/he may find a more dramatic means of pushing off. Parents of straight and gay children alike must recognize that yesterday's ear piercing is today's tongue piercing. Sometimes, for the greater good, you must grin and bear it!

IDENTITY SYNTHESIS

The experience: When the LGBTQ at this stage thinks about himself, being gay is just one of many aspects of who he is. In the past, he might have felt like he was walking around wearing a big sign announcing himself as "GAY" or "QUEER." That sign is gone now. This individual sometimes thinks about being gay, but not every day like he used to. He no longer views the heterosexual community as all bad and the gay community as all good. His grounded sense of self has made him less reactive to homophobic people and remarks. He finds that he can confront homophobia more successfully because he feels less vulnerable. There is a sense that life can now move forward without the internal fears and anxiety that previously devoured his energy. He no longer has one identity for the heterosexual world and another for the gay world. He has a single identity and it's good enough for all.

The discussion: It is my observation that those who work through the coming out process and arrive at Identity Synthesis have grown in dramatic ways. Having had no script to follow, they created their own stories and chose their own destinies. They discovered in themselves the resiliency to survive when it felt like all the world was against them. They learned that bad times, even horrible times, do pass with patience. They learned how strong they can be and that integrity and dignity are impregnable. No person, no group, no state, no nation can strip them of these things. At this point in a gay person's life, the lessons learned from being gay are worth all the trouble they have caused in the learning of them.

Cass's stages depict general phases through which a gay person moves as s/he integrates sexual identity. Sexual identity development does not occur in isolation from other developmental processes. It occurs concomitantly with social-emotional development, physical development, cognitive development and moral development. All these processes interact with one another in complex ways. It is also a process that occurs within social contexts, both favorable and unfavorable, and those contexts influence development.

Despite these complexities, I have found this model useful in helping gay clients though the coming out process. It helps a client to mark where he or she is and to engage in efforts that will move him or her toward an integrated sense of self. I have also found that those within the relational circle of a gay person's life can benefit from understanding this model. As a parent, it may help you better interpret your child's reactions and behavior.

Here is an illustrative example: Jim, a member of a local youth organization, and his dad were selling candy door-to-door as a fundraiser for the organization. They went to Greg's house and he bought a few bars. After Greg shut the door, Greg's gay son Bobby told him, "The people in that organization are bigots and you shouldn't support them." Greg asked why and Bobby told him that they prohibit gays from joining the group or serving as leaders. Greg exclaimed, "Oh, I know Jim's father and he wouldn't do anything like that." Bobby told him that Jim's father was discriminating by putting his son in the group and that Greg was discriminating by supporting the group through his purchase. Bobby marched off angrily to his room while Greg stood there in a state of utter confusion.

The son's reaction is understandable. He's been learning about discrimination and he knows that the youth organization has gone to court to defend its homophobic policies. At this point, Bobby is between the stages of Identity Acceptance and Identity Pride. He is still a novice in managing the pain of oppression and he is furious that he is oppressed at all. He doesn't know how to fight back. From an emotional standpoint, he might experience this episode as the equivalent of someone calling him a faggot. Or he might perceive it as worse, because Greg minimized the discrimination.

If you were Bobby's father you would need to understand that, at this time, he needs you to listen. Ask him to tell you about the organization and what it did to its gay members. Empathize. Try to assure him that you support him and that you don't believe that someone should be excluded from a group because he is gay. Ask what you can do to help. Maybe the two of you can write a letter to the organization together. Whatever you do, don't minimize discrimination.

Eventually, your son will learn to choose his battles so they don't exhaust him. He will recognize that his battles are not always your battles. He will come to understand that your experience of something is different from his experience of the same thing because you are a different person and because you are not gay. Even if you are gay, you might not feel the same as him and react in the same way to a particular type of discrimination.

Eventually, your child will learn that it is unfair to ask you to be an extension of him. When that time comes, he will be delighted when you take action to support gay rights, but he will also have learned to tolerate when you miss the mark or have a difference of opinion, as long as he feels loved and accepted by you.

··

Chapter 18

When Development Derails

As children approach adulthood, the parent-child relationship can change in dramatic ways. Parents gradually surrender the authority that gave them the right to set limits and hold their children accountable. They accept a very different role with limited power: that of advisor and counselor. Failure to make this shift will strain the parent-child relationship and thwart maturation. A young adult who is kept on a "short leash" will either submit or try to break free. If s/he pulls and breaks free, s/he will likely be propelled far away, at a safe distance beyond parental reach and influence. If s/he submits, the child will fail to meet and conquer the developmental challenges of young adulthood that can only be encountered beyond the bounds of parental supervision. Neither of these options are healthy ones. Painful as it may be, frightening as it may be, parents must let go and let their children grow and become independent. Only after a child sees that his or her parents respect his or her independence can s/he safely use them as a touchstone for consolation and advice. Accepting your child's sexual identity is necessary for his or her continued emotional development, but it is also necessary for the successful transition from the parent-child relationship to a parent-adult child relationship.

The relinquishing of parental control comes in stages. In early adolescence, you need to encourage your child to make minor decisions, such as clothing, length of hair and whether to join a sports team or try out for the school play. By late adolescence, your child should be making decisions that have more lasting consequences, such as whether to go to college or get a job and whether to say yes or no to sex with a partner. Eventually, as the child becomes an adult, the child should assume full responsibility for his or her decisions. When that happens, the child becomes a full-fledged adult. The age at which adulthood commences is not set in stone, but a good estimate is somewhere between eighteen and twenty-two years of age.

Failure to separate from parents leaves a young adult psychologically tethered to them. Not only does this limit psychosocial development, but also it puts a strain on the parent-child relationship. Any small conflict can feel like a tug-of-war.

Family systems psychologists (among them Salvador Minuchin, Virginia Satir and Murray Bowen) have developed and popularized approaches to family therapy that focus on issues such as the importance of boundaries between family members. In healthy families, individuals maintain and respect boundaries while maintaining connection. When a family member's boundaries are too rigid, family systems therapists refer to the relationship as *disengaged*. When a family member's boundaries are too permeable, family systems therapists refer to this relationship as *enmeshed*. Boundary problems in a family can delay, halt or distort normal child development. When a child is gay, parent-child boundary problems add yet another layer of complication to sexual identity development, a process already burdened by homophobia.[1]

In working with LGBTQ adolescents, the problem of overly permeable boundaries is significant. I've had gay adolescent and young adult clients whose parents not only rejected the children's sexual orientations but also used whatever leverage they may have had to discourage the children's relationships.

It can perhaps be hard to comprehend how a parent and child can be too close. Clasp your hands together so that the fingers of each hand interlock alternately. Notice that it can be difficult to tell, just by looking, which fingers belong to which hand. Similarly, when two people are enmeshed, they find it hard to determine which decisions belong to whom. When your hands are clasped, it's hard to see that they are two separate parts and not one whole. Now try to move one hand. This drags the other hand along with it. In enmeshed relationships, conflicts are emotionally charged. Because the parties involved are entangled, movement by one party disrupts the other.

Another way to think about enmeshed relationships is to think about power. When identities become entangled, struggles over personal power occur. Often it appears as though one person gives his or her power to another and, right after doing so, begins a fight to get it back. Here's an example: Keith tells his mother that he's going to the park to play basketball. His mom says she doesn't want him to go out because he has bad sunburn. Keith tells her he'll wear sunblock, but his mother insists that he stay inside. Keith, who was on his way out the door, turns around and slams the door shut. He plops down on the couch and begins a long rant, "Mom, I'm seventeen years old. When are you going to stop telling me when and if I can go out! You hover over me like I'm a five-year-old kid! None of my other friends have a mother like that!" In this case, Keith's mom doesn't recognize she is overstepping and Keith doesn't realize that he need not let her. Keith could have said, "Thanks for the tip, Mom. See you later," but instead Keith assumes the role of a young child. He does what he is told and then whines about it. Adults and young adults who forfeit their power run the risk of never fully assuming control of it. Adolescent power has limits while the teen remains a minor and under his or her parents' guardianship.

LGBTQs who anticipate parental disapproval might decide to delay coming out. Those who are enmeshed with their parents might feel that such an announcement would be doomed to provoke a powerful, even explosive parental reaction. If this occurs, the enmeshed child is likely to respond with equal intensity, either imploding (depression and suicide) or exploding (intense anger directed toward the parents).

Because there is not a clear boundary between self and other, enmeshed parents are at risk for commenting without editing. If they have not dealt with their homophobia, they may say deeply hurtful things. In addition, they are likely to try to assert control over decisions that should be left to the child, such as when to disclose, to whom to disclose and even whom to date.

Dr. Laurie Heatherington of Williams College and Justin Lavner of the University of California, Los Angeles, reviewed family systems therapists' opinions about coming out. They found that positive parental reactions to coming out are associated with fewer negative feelings about a child's growing autonomy and more positive feelings about the parent-child relationship (feelings of closeness and empathy).[2] Similarly, LGBs who report more secure attachments to parents as measured by the effective quality of the attachment, parental fostering of autonomy and parental emotional support are more likely to be out and to be out for a longer period of time to their parents and are less likely to report depressive thoughts about self, others and the future.[3] Heatherington and Lavner explain that negative parental reactions to coming out can hinder a child's efforts in attaining autonomy (which is necessary for identity development) while remaining emotionally connected to parents.

For these reasons I've cited, it is important for parents to recognize the line that separates them from their children. In young adulthood, that line is relatively new. One may think of it as drawn in chalk, where it can be rethought, scratched out and drawn again. If you can't find the boundary between you and your teenage child, sit down together and map one out. If attempts to talk calmly and respectfully about differences degrade into arguments and hurt feelings, consider obtaining the guidance of a family therapist to help re-chart the parent-child relationship and develop a new rapport.

Let's return to Keith's situation and add sexual orientation. Keith and his parents attend a church that preaches against homosexuality. Keith is painfully aware of this because, for several years, he's been fighting homosexual feelings. The harder he fights the feelings, the stronger they become, until it is all he can think about. He feels he has to tell someone. His father is more conservative than his mother, so he decides to tell his mother. For all their bickering, he knows she loves him. When he tells his mom, "I think I'm gay," she takes him to the preacher. Together they tell Keith's father, who is no happier than Keith's mother to hear the news. The family and preacher talk and pray together until Keith convinces them that the "problem" is resolved.

Keith begins attending college and he and another student fall in love. This time, Keith knows better than to tell his parents, but Keith's parents visit Keith's dormitory without calling first and find Keith and his partner kissing. This ignites a loud, tearful argument.

When Keith is twenty years old and in his third year of college, his dad has softened a bit. He even asks Keith's partner to come along when they go out to lunch. Keith's mom is polite, but not welcoming. While Keith's mom has reluctantly accepted Keith's homosexuality, she manages to work comments into the conversation such as, "Keith is going to do what Keith wants to do regardless of how it affects the rest of us." These comments bother Keith's partner, but Keith ignores what his mother says. When Keith's mother comments that the gay rights sticker on Keith's car is an invitation to get beaten up, Keith removes it, saying, "It's only a sticker!" His partner says, "No. It's about a lot more than a sticker."

The boyfriend is right! Keith's mom and Keith are enmeshed. Keith's failure to individuate or separate from his mother stunts his growth. At this age he should be asserting his identity. He should be able to stand up for himself and for what is important to him. If he can't break away from his mother, he will likely have difficulty facing the next stages of social-emotional development. Keith's enmeshment with his mother is interfering with his relationship with his partner. Removing the gay rights sticker from his car suggests that Keith's unhealthy relationship with his mother is chipping away at his integrity.

Allowing your child to separate from you will not diminish your connection with your child. Instead it will allow for a new connection, one based on mutual love and respect. While young children require parental supervision and intervention, young adults don't. They require room to grow. If given that room, they will want to share their adventures with you. Your child may not always need your permission or want your advice, but he or she will always need your love.

······································
Resiliency and Hope

History is replete with examples of individuals who shined a light in the darkness and changed history. Leaders like Martin Luther King Jr., Mahatma Gandhi and Mother Teresa offered visions that countered oppression, but hope can operate at the micro level too. Hope is the gay boy who sticks it out through high school despite being harassed, because he wants to go to college. Hope is the lesbian girl who says no to drugs when the parking lot is full of opportunities to get high and forget about being bullied. Hope is the bisexual child who risks ridicule by starting a Gay-Straight Alliance at his school. Psychologists describe people like this as *resilient*.

Resilient people bend without breaking. They recover better and more quickly from emotional injury. If the oppression is a crushing weight, then resiliency is a coiled spring that bears the weight most effectively and efficiently.

Dr. Cecily Knight, a longtime researcher of children's social-emotional development, says that resiliency has three components: emotional competence, social competence and futures-orientation.[1] Emotional competence is having good self-esteem, being autonomous and having a sense of humor. People with emotional competence also believe that they are in control, rather than believing that they are victims to forces outside of themselves—having an internal locus of control rather than an external locus of control. People who are socially competent have good communication skills, empathy and a benevolent stance toward others. This helps them maintain supportive relationships that serve to insulate them from negative influences. Futures-oriented individuals are optimistic, spiritually grounded, critical thinkers, flexible, adaptive and proactive. In essence, they are good problem-solvers. They use these skills to set goals and move toward goal completion. This gives their lives meaning and purpose.

Resiliency is associated with connectedness to school and family. When children feel safe in a setting and when they feel supported at school and at home they are less likely to suffer from depression and less likely to commit suicide.[2] In fact, family and school connectedness may reduce the risk of teen pregnancy.[3]

Researchers have begun to study how having the quality of resiliency affects LGBTQs as they function, meet obstacles and mature. They have found that resilient LGBTQs do a number of things better than their less resilient counterparts:

- **Resilient LGBTQs make friends with other sexual minorities**.[4] Gay youths need a range of relationships to help them successfully manage stigmatization, oppression and bullying. Those who have gay-affirming family and friends fare better than those who have family and friends who reject them because of their sexual orientations. A lack of family support is associated with higher rates of depression and attempted suicide. It is not enough for family to be supportive about other aspects of an LGBTQ's personality. LGBTQs need support specifically related to LGBTQ issues if they are to manage sexual minority stressors. The opportunity to develop friendships with gay peers is important for all gay youths but especially for those who don't get support at home or from heterosexual friends.

- **Resilient LGBTQs cope with mental health issues before they multiply**.[5] Adversity experienced in adolescence, such as discrimination, increases the risk of depression, anxiety, substance use and participation in unsafe sexual behavior in later life. When these problems co-occur, they have a synergistic effect on one another. The greater the number

of psychosocial problems, the more likely gay men are to
engage in unsafe sex and the more likely they are to be
infected with HIV.

- **Resilient homeless LGBTQs display certain survival skills.**[6]
  - They avoid fights and conflicts with police.
  - They are able to identify safe locations, places to sleep
    and places to go in bad weather.
  - They are able to get around, get the things they need
    and find food without having money.
  - When they need money, they find a way to get some.
  - They are able to deal with agencies and services.
  - They identify and avoid people who might steal from
    them.
  - They identify and keep in touch with people who will
    look out for them and people from whom they can learn.

Researchers found that, unfortunately, after six months
on the street, these resilient behaviors begin to degrade. More
work is needed to explore how survival strategies can be supported, maintained and perhaps taught to homeless children.

- **Resilient LGBTQs are psychologically prepared to come
  out.**[7] Coming out is consistently associated with mental
  health benefits, but adolescents who come out need to
  be ready and need to have supports in place. Suicide
  attempts are highest among gay adolescents within the first
  year of coming out. For each year's delay in homosexual
  self-labeling, the odds of a suicide attempt decrease by
  80 percent. This tells us that early adolescents may have
  a harder time coping with stigma, discrimination and
  rejection than older adolescents and adults. If your child has
  come to a resolution about his or her sexuality during early
  adolescence, you should be vigilant for how important people
  react to his or her coming out. A positive reaction from
  parents goes a long way.

Peer reactions matter as well. When I was coming out, a
wise gay friend told me that my discovery that I was gay was
a gift to myself and that I could enjoy that gift, privately, for

as long as I needed or wanted before sharing it with anyone else. Ultimately, coming out is a healthy choice, but one has to be psychologically prepared to manage reactions. If your child is struggling with negative feelings about being gay, it may be best to delay coming out to some or all people until self-esteem is stable.

- **Resilient religious LGBTQs find supportive spiritual homes**.[8] Gays who belong to religions that view homosexuality as sinful tend to suffer more psychological distress than those who belong to gay-affirming religions. In addition, a gay-friendly environment encourages LGBTQs to come out of the closet and benefit from the support a religious community has to offer. For those whose childhood faiths condemned sexual orientation, being a part of an accepting faith community can be tremendously healing.

The goal of the oppressor is to extinguish hope. Once hope is snuffed out, it is easy to get people to submit to whatever treatment is given them. Once hope is gone, there is no reason to set goals or plan a future, because there is no future. Be sure that your child never loses sight of the good things that life has to offer. Encourage him or her to trudge on, even if the present is fraught with difficulty. As long as your child maintains an eye on the future, s/he will be able to endure what comes his or her way today. By the way, hope is catching. If one person has hope, he can breathe it into many. If many have hope, they can change the way the wind blows.

PART IV
HEALTH AND SEXUALITY

Chapter 20

Sexuality: The Birds and the Bees Revisited

It's difficult to say what percentage of the population is gay. Even when surveyors promise anonymity, LGBs who hide their identities may lie about sexual orientation due to fear of being outed. People who engage in same-sex relationships but identify as queer may resist being labeled as lesbian, gay or bisexual. Famed tennis player Martina Navratilova, a homosexual, commented, "Labels are for filing. Labels are for clothing. Labels are not for people." Those who suffer from high levels of internalized homophobia may deny their sexual orientations even though they experience same-sex attractions. It's important to keep these limitations in mind when considering the accuracy of sexual minority population estimates.

According to the National Health and Social Life Survey and the General Social Survey, 4.7 percent of adult men and 3.6 percent of adult women have had at least one same-sex partner since age eighteen. When asked about their current relationships, 2.5 percent of men and 1.4 percent of women reported having same-sex partners within the past year.[1] While these statistics reflect relationship status, they don't indicate sexual activity outside of relationships nor do they include gays and lesbians who are not in relationships but who nonetheless identify as LGBTQ. There were no general population-based studies on the prevalence of transgender orientation as of 2011, though one large Internet survey found that 0.2 percent of respondents described themselves as transgender.[2]

For more detailed estimates of homosexuality and homosexual behavior across the lifespan, we turn to the work of American biologist Alfred Kinsey. His works, *Sexual Behavior in the Human Male* and *Sexual Behavior in the Human Female*, published over sixty years ago, were best sellers and are still regarded as perhaps the finest research on sexuality to date. At a time when sex was not considered an appropriate topic for conversation, Kinsey and his colleagues conducted face-to-face interviews with a cross section of the United States population, twelve thousand men and eight thousand women, asking detailed questions about sexual behavior. He then had the temerity to publish the results.

According to Kinsey's findings, about 4 percent of US males and 2 to 3 percent of US females reported having exclusively same-sex partners throughout their entire lives. About 8 percent of males reported having sex with only men for a period lasting at least three years. Kinsey estimated that somewhere between 3 to 10 percent of the US population is engaged primarily in homosexual activity at any point in time. Until this point, it was supposed that homosexuality was rather rare in nature. Kinsey, an animal biologist by training, knew this to be untrue:

> The impression that infra-human mammals more or less confine themselves to heterosexual activities is a distortion of fact which appears to have originated in a man-made philosophy, rather than in specific observations of mammalian behavior...Sexual contacts between individuals of the same sex are known to occur in practically every species of mammal which has been extensively studied. In many species, homosexual contacts occur with considerable frequency...Every farmer who has raised cattle knows, for instance, that cows quite regularly mount cows.[3]

Perhaps most astonishing, Kinsey found 50 percent of the male population surveyed was exclusively heterosexual throughout adult life, about 4 percent were exclusively homosexual and nearly half,

46 percent, engaged in both heterosexual and homosexual activity or reacted sexually to persons of both sexes in the course of their lives. In fact, 37 percent of all the men surveyed and about 12 to 13 percent of the women surveyed reported having a same-sex sexual encounter resulting in orgasm at some point in their lives.

Based on these findings, Kinsey concluded that there was no "homosexual personality."

Instead, homosexuality was a part of normal sexual behavior for a large portion of the population. In addition, he argued that sexual activity was more fluid and changing than previously described. Homosexual and heterosexual, he asserted, were adjectives, not nouns:

> The world is not to be divided into sheep and goats. Not all things are black nor all things white. It is a fundamental of taxonomy that nature rarely deals with discrete categories. Only the human mind invents categories and tries to force facts into separated pigeon-holes. The living world is a continuum in each and every one of its aspects. The sooner we learn this concerning human sexual behavior, the sooner we shall reach a sound understanding of the realities of sex.[4]

To capture the observed range of sexual orientation, he developed the Kinsey Scale. On the Kinsey Scale, one can fall anywhere on a continuum between 0, extremely heterosexual, to 6, extremely homosexual, with degrees of bisexuality falling between the two extremes. Kinsey's successors at the Kinsey Institute have suggested some changes to the scale, such as adding separate scale factors for love, sexual attraction, fantasy and self-identification. They also point out that sexual orientation may change over time and that those who use the scale should not see an individual's score as predictive of his or her future sexual behavior or sexual identity.[5] The scale, perhaps with a few alterations, is still in use today.

Some people found Kinsey's work offensive. Political pressures ensued and Kinsey lost his funding. He died shortly thereafter, in 1956, but not without making his mark. Kinsey's work unveiled a hidden world of sexual behavior.

Among those who followed Kinsey and his work was Shere Hite. Like Kinsey, Hite surveyed a massive swath of the US public. Unlike Kinsey, she used an anonymous written questionnaire. She presented her results to the public in essay form, rather than Kinsey's quantitative approach, relying heavily on quotations from the study participants.[6]

Though her survey took place several decades after Kinsey's, her results are quite similar to Kinsey's findings. She found 43 percent of men surveyed had same-sex encounters in their youth.[7] The occurrence of a same-sex encounter did not predict sexual orientation later in life. In terms of population estimates for homosexuality, Hite reported that 11 percent of men preferred sex with men; of that 11 percent, two percent also had sex with women.[8]

Because of Hite's style of reporting results, we have the unique opportunity to hear from many individual men directly. Reading their words, it seems that the adolescent openness to same-sex connections has been replaced by a radical homophobia. When Hite asked, "Do you embrace or kiss men in friendship?" the overwhelming answer was no. Here are few of the responses:[9]

- "I can't bear any kind of physical intimacy with a man beyond just shaking hands and that feels clammy enough to me."
- "I may be the victim of hang-ups, but I really cannot stand even being touched by another male (except for an occasional handshake)."
- "I only embrace my father and I don't really like it."
- "Any guy tries to kiss me and I'll bite his tongue off."

The degree of expressed repulsion in regard to male-male expressions of affection strongly suggests denial of earlier same-sex attraction and activity. If it were not denial and instead a true lack of desire for male-male affection, then the response would be one of indifference or neutrality and not nearly so extreme. This is upsetting, but it is no great surprise. Western culture places great restrictions on men in terms of gender conformity. Because homosexuality is often thought of as equivalent to gender nonconformity, men are conditioned, early on, to suppress anything that comes close to feelings of same-sex attraction. This expectation is so severe, so extreme, that there are those who cannot even hug a friend or their fathers without triggering that conditioned repulsion.

Hite found that about 83 percent of women surveyed preferred sex with men, 8 percent preferred sex with women and 9 percent did not express a preference. She says that many women who had never had a same-sex encounter were curious and interested in having one. Hite found that the women surveyed were less reactive than men to the idea of displaying affection toward members of the same sex and less defensive about experiencing feelings of arousal that may spontaneously occur when doing so:[10]

- "There are times when I feel such a warmth from my best friend that I experience it sexually and almost desire her."
- "I want a woman lover—or more. I generally want closer relationships with women; I want to do all the things only men are supposed to do! I want to explore!"
- "I have never had sex with a woman and can't imagine it, but that is because of my conditioning. I can see why women would want other women and can accept it. I don't know any lesbians that I know of. I have a close girlfriend who is divorced and we have discussed this a little and it seems we are both 'straight' but I notice we never touch each other. Are we afraid we might be gay and couldn't handle it?"

I am struck by Hite's consistency with Kinsey's earlier findings, spanning many decades. The existence of homosexuality has been a well-kept secret. The fact that this secrecy is breaking in my lifetime is quite a thrill. The fact that it is breaking in your son's or daughter's lifetime puts your child in a historically unique position. Today's children will be the architects of a new reality for gays and lesbians.

Ava's Story

Ava is twelve years old. One night over dinner, Ava announced that she was queer. Her dad asked her what that meant and Ava responded she wasn't sure. Her dad replied, "How can you be queer if you don't even know what it is?" Ava stormed off, leaving her dad baffled. Ava was always flirting with boys, but she did have one really close girl friend. Ava's father wondered if something was going on between the two girls.

Today, children learn about sex much earlier than past generations did. They also engage in sexual activity earlier. Frankly, I wish there were a way to slow it all down. Sex is a powerful thing. It can promote a level of intimacy that is unmanageable for the young and emotionally immature. It can get one sick, if one is not yet assertive enough to demand safe sex. It can get one pregnant. However, sex is a beautiful thing for those who are self-aware, assertive and mature enough not to be thrown off by its wondrous intensity.

Ava is only twelve, but in the United States and many other countries today she is well within the age range of considering sex and sexuality. However, I advised her father not to jump to conclusions about what was happening. There were many possibilities. Ava may be attracted to boys. She may not be attracted to boys but pretending in order to fit in. She may be attracted to her girl friend. She may have cuddled with or kissed her girl friend. She may be attracted to both boys and her girl friend. She may not understand her feelings toward boys or toward her girl friend. She may not yet know to whom she's attracted and be experimenting with her sexuality. She may be asserting her independence from all labels by defining herself as queer. She may not have an idea of what queer means.

Ava's father needs to find a book which explores same-sex relationships. The publishers of the standby *Our Bodies, Ourselves* now publish books about sex and sexuality for girls at various ages and I recommend them as resources. I also advised this parent against drawing premature conclusions about Ava's sexual orientation. Sexual behavior, especially at this age, is not necessarily an indicator of sexual orientation. Ava is only twelve. Her true sexual orientation will surface in due time. In the meantime, her dad should maintain an interested and nonjudgmental tone that encourages open and honest communication, one that encourages his daughter to discover her sexual self safely, slowly and freely.

Remember, fathers can talk to daughters about sex and moms can talk to sons. If you're a single parent or part of a same-sex couple, don't assume you're at a disadvantage when it comes time to have a talk about sexual relationships. The gender of the parent is less important than the quality of the parenting. In most cases, children will gravitate toward adults whom they anticipate will be the least judgmental and most comfortable with conversations of this nature.

The next chapters discuss LGBT health disparities. The impact of minority status, if you are not already familiar with it, has been staggering and sad. As you read, remember that your child is part of the first generation to live in a society that recognizes the existence of homosexuality and the issue of gay rights. This will confer great health benefits, at least to those who live in towns, cities and states that support gay rights. I predict that researchers who write about the health of gay men and women ten and twenty years from now will have great news. They will discover that gays, in general, have suffered from fewer health disparities than their predecessors. They will find that gays living in the most gay-friendly states will have had better access to health care and will have suffered fewer health disparities compared to gays living in less gay-friendly states. They will conclude that when the law lifts the weight of oppression from our children's shoulders, they will live healthier lives. The big changes begin with your children.

Many variables confound the attempts of researchers who try to understand the experience of sexual minorities. First, sexual orientation and gender identity are not listed on many state and national surveys. Second, sexual behavior doesn't always coincide neatly with sexual identity. For example, some people who identify as lesbians also have sex with men. Third, fear of disclosing sexual minority status makes it impossible to generalize results of studies with absolute confidence. Despite the limited data, here is a summary of LGB health risks, transgender health issues and suggestions of how you can help. Later we'll discuss ways to optimize health care.

LGB HEALTH RISKS

Social stigmatization and discrimination are sources of chronic stress that take a toll on health. In a review of literature, Dr. Elizabeth Pascoe, assistant professor of psychological sciences at the University of Northern Colorado, and Dr. Laura Smart Richman, assistant professor of psychology and neuroscience at Duke University, explain that chronic stress and the associated autonomic arousal cause wear and tear on the body which results in greater vulnerability to disease. This wear and tear also manifests in psychological exhaustion which

increases participation in unhealthy behaviors and decreases participation in healthy behaviors.[1]

Columbia University researchers Ilan Meyer, Jessica Dietrich and
Sharon Schwartz delineate the stressors into two broad types: distal
stressors and proximal stressors. Distal stressors are direct effects of
discrimination and prejudice, like being the victim of a hate crime or
being exposed to negative comments about one's sexuality. Proximal
stressors occur internally as a function of internalized homophobia,
such as someone believing he is a bad person because he is gay or hiding
his sexual orientation.[2]

Disadvantaged social status adds to this burden. As Meyer,
Dietrich and Schwartz explain, those at the lower ends of the social
strata not only experience more stressors but also have less access
to resources to deal with those stressors. For example, if a person is
denied a job because she is gay, she experiences the emotional pain
of being discriminated against but also the fiscal pain of being out of
work. If she is ultimately unable to find a job due to discrimination,
she will experience all the disadvantages that accompany poverty.
It would help if she could join a gym to work off the stress, but she
doesn't have the money. If stress results in illness, she doesn't have
health insurance and so her health needs go unmet. In this way, disad-
vantaged social status compounds the negative effects of oppression.[3]

As a result of discrimination, stigmatization and isolation, LGBs
are at increased risk for depression, anxiety, drug and alcohol abuse,
smoking, obesity, low self-esteem, suicide and sexually transmitted
diseases.[4] As already discussed, LGBs are at risk of being bullied in the
school environment. Physical and verbal victimization is a common
experience for LGBTQs and the resulting trauma has lasting negative effects to mental health, such as increased risk for post-traumatic
stress disorder.

In a review of the literature, clinical psychologist Dr. Michael
Marshal and a panel of his peers report much higher rates of substance
use in LGB adolescents.[5] Compared to heterosexual youths, LGB adolescents are 190 percent more likely to use substances, with the highest use among bisexuals and female sexual minorities, 340 percent
and 400 percent higher than for heterosexual youths, respectively. A
large national study of LGBs twenty years and older confirmed previous findings of higher rates of substance dependence among LGBs;

however, most LGBs were not substance dependent and there was considerable variability in use based on gender and how sexual orientation was defined.[6]

One systematic national review of smoking in sexual minorities noted higher rates in sexual minorities who identified as "mostly homosexual" as compared to those who identified as "homosexual" and higher rates among those who had sex with both men and women as compared to those having exclusive, same-sex relationships.[7] Whether this reflects higher rates of smoking among bisexuals as compared to gays and lesbians or whether it reflects increased rates of smoking associated with incomplete sexual identity development is not clear.

Lesbians and bisexual women are at increased risk for being overweight and obese.[8] One study of college women found that lesbians were 1.73 times more likely and bisexual women 1.53 times more likely to be overweight or obese than their heterosexual peers.[9] Gay male adolescents and gay men do not appear to have an increased risk for obesity and may actually have lower rates of obesity than their heterosexual counterparts. Contrary to popular myth, there is no association between weight and high risk sexual behavior in gay men.[10]

LGBTQ youths are vastly overrepresented among runaways living on the street. As many as 25 to 40 percent of youths on the street identify as LGBTQs. Parental rejection is one contributing factor to this percentage. Gay runaways are sometimes referred to as "throwaways." Discrimination is another factor. In one study of city runaways, 80 percent reported that emotional turmoil resulting from exposure to ridiculing jokes and negative stereotypes was a primary reason for leaving school and home. When living on the street, LGBTQs fare worse than their heterosexual peers. For instance, they are more likely than heterosexual runaways to resort to prostitution for survival.

Girls who identify as lesbian and bisexual are just as likely as their heterosexual peers to have intercourse (a common finding), but are 12 percent more likely to become pregnant and more likely to engage in prostitution.[11] This may sound counterintuitive, but one of the profound effects of oppression is a collapse of self-care. Safe sex often depends on a girl's self-esteem and her desire for self-preservation. Additionally, homelessness is greater among LGBs and homelessness is associated with survival sex.

Because sexual orientation is not listed on death records and because it is often impossible to know why a person commits suicide, there is no reliable way to estimate completed suicides among the LGBTQ population. Information on suicide attempts, however, is available. Since population-based surveys of adolescents began to ask about sexual orientation in the 1990s, the rate of reported suicide attempts among LGBs has been two to seven times higher than the rate of suicide attempts among heterosexual adolescents.[12] One study that looked at suicide method found that more than half of the attempts involved potentially lethal methods and 21 percent of attempts resulted in a medical or psychiatric hospitalization.[13]

As would be expected, a number of factors play a mediating role in suicidal behavior. Having a mental health disorder increases the risk of suicidal behavior.[14] A meta-analysis of twenty-five international and national studies of LGB adolescents and adults found that certain mental health disorders (depression, anxiety disorders and substance use disorders) were 1.5 times more common in LGBs than in heterosexuals.[15]

Other factors that can increase the likelihood of suicidal behavior include environmental stressors such as victimization or a recent suicide attempt by a family member or peer.[16] Homelessness, with all its inherent difficulties and its association with parental rejection, is a critical mediating factor. In one study, 53 percent of gay homeless youths had attempted suicide.[17]

Suicide risk is highest during youth and adolescence, but it is unclear if this elevation is directly related to age or if it reflects an in-creased risk during the early stages of coming out. Among LGB adolescents, African American males appear to be at greatest risk of attempting suicide. Among LGB adults, the highest rates of suicide are among men with lower socioeconomic status and among Latinos and Asian Americans. Overall, gay and bisexual men are more likely to attempt suicide than lesbian and bisexual women.[18]

· ·

Jamie's Story

Jamie, a sixteen-year-old high school student, recently came out as a lesbian and entered a relationship with Jennifer. After Jennifer broke up with her,

Jamie found several partially used bottles of pills in her parents' medicine cabinet and took them with a large amount of wine. Her parents returned home from work a half an hour later and found Jamie passed out on the living room floor. They took her to the hospital where doctors pumped out her stomach.

There is nothing more frightening for a parent than a child's suicide attempt. Jamie's attempt, though spontaneous, was serious. Parents should not assume that, because their child could anticipate being discovered and rescued, the attempt was not serious.

Psychologists consider degree of planning, method used, access to method and potential lethality of method when assessing a person's suicidal thinking. They also consider factors that have been associated with an increased risk of suicide, such as having a family history of suicide, recent exposure to a peer's suicide, previous suicide attempts, substance abuse or drug dependence, mood disorder, head injury with disinhibition, chronic pain and chronic illness. Being gay, young and in the early stages of coming out are also risk factors, as is a recent breakup. Adolescents lack the coping skills to deal with intense grief and they lack the experience to know that the pain they feel will eventually pass.

In most cases, such an attempt would result in admission to a hospital's psychiatric unit after medical stabilization. After Jamie was discharged from the hospital, I advised Jamie's parents to insist that she attend sessions with a qualified, gay-friendly therapist for counseling until that provider, in this case me, felt comfortable that Jamie's thoughts and feelings had stabilized. As Jamie's psychologist, I screened her for mental health disorders, including substance dependence. It is important that parents not take any attempt at self-harm lightly.

••

TRANSGENDER HEALTH CONCERNS

The National Gay and Lesbian Task Force and the National Center for Transgender Equality released the results of the National Transgender Discrimination Survey in 2011. This survey explored the health and well-being of 6,450 transgender and gender-nonconforming people across the United States. The results are deeply disturbing. Of the respondents, 51 percent reported being harassed or bullied in school,

61 percent were victims of physical assault and 55 percent reported losing a job due to bias. Respondents were almost four times more likely to live in extreme poverty when compared to the general population. Of those surveyed, 41 percent reported attempting suicide.

Those who reported gender nonconformity during kindergarten through high school reported being harassed (78 percent), physically assaulted (35 percent) and sexually assaulted (12 percent). A total of 15 percent of respondents said they dropped out of school due to harassment at some point in their lives. Respondents who identified as non-white, especially those who identified as African American, fared worse on most measures when compared to their Caucasian counterparts. The desire for hormonal reassignment was strong and constant. Even though access to health care was a barrier, 76 percent of transgender people surveyed received hormone therapy; 78 percent felt more comfortable at work and felt their performance improved after transitioning, despite the fact that harassment continued.[19]

According to a meta-analysis of twenty-nine studies, 27.7 percent of male-to-female transgender persons were infected with HIV.[20] Higher rates were found among African Americans. (The prevalence of HIV infection in female-to-male transgender persons was low.) Those transgender people infected with HIV often had mental health concerns, histories of physical abuse and unmet transgender-specific healthcare needs. They also experienced economic problems and social isolation.

The National Transgender Discrimination Survey offers evidence that family support can mitigate the negative effects of discrimination experienced by transgender individuals. While most transgender people reported experiencing significant family rejection (57 percent), those who maintained family bonds (43 percent) were less likely to contract HIV, less likely to experience homelessness, less likely to be incarcerated, less likely to engage in sex work or other underground work for income, less likely to smoke, less likely to use drugs or alcohol to cope with mistreatment and less likely to attempt suicide.

WHAT CAN PARENTS DO?

Your adjustment to your child's gender orientation may be difficult, but be aware your child's adjustment is greater. Support your child. Be reassured that, in time, whatever awkwardness or foreignness you may feel will subside. Regardless of his or her gender, your child needs your love.

Too many transgender children kill themselves or sacrifice themselves to the streets because they cannot bear the pain of being transgender or because they cannot bear the abuse they receive because of their gender orientations. If your child is transgender, there are some steps you can take that will improve his or her odds. School personnel and police need to be better trained on issues that affect transgender youths; as a parent, you're entitled to be the vocal advocate who makes it happen.

You can also help your child connect with other transgender youths through gay alliance groups in your town. Organizations like PFLAG may be able to offer suggestions. You can contact the Gay, Lesbian and Straight Education Network (GLSEN), which works with teachers, parents and students to improve the educational environment for LGBTQs by addressing issues related to harassment. Groups like GLSEN, PFLAG and Straight-Gay Alliance will give your child a chance to work through negative feelings, dissemble stereotypes and build a healthy self-esteem.

FOSTER EMOTIONAL HEALTH

Emotional health is, in my opinion, the cornerstone of overall well-being. I treat individuals who suffer from chronic disease but relish life because, though physically in pain or impaired, they are emotionally sound. I also treat clients in good health who, due to emotional problems, suffer anxiety and depression each passing day. While maintenance of all aspects of well-being is the goal, attention to emotional health will likely lead to improved self-care and general well-being.

What is the basis of emotional health? Good self-esteem is a key component. Intrapersonal awareness, the awareness and ability to identify one's feelings, is another. While important to any child's emotional health, LGBTQ children need an extra dose of each to help them manage the challenges they are bound to face. Sometimes the challenges life imposes make a person more confident. Involvement in gay-affirmative groups and exposure to important gay-positive role models can transform emotional challenges into emotional triumphs. Many of the people I admire most are those who have struggled against one obstacle or another to survive and live fulfilling lives.

Emotional health also requires identifying and treating a mood or anxiety disorder at the earliest possible stage. The word *depression* implies to de-press, to push down. Depression is often the pushing down and away of feelings that are either too unacceptable or too painful to confront. As discussed earlier, the first stages of sexual identity development for gays are full of angst. Most people recognize that they are gay before believing that being gay is acceptable. As a result, sexual feelings are pushed down and away and self-esteem takes a hit. The tendency for depression subsides as an individual passes through the early stages of conflict and into Identity Pride, which, by its label, announces the return of unfettered self-esteem.

It is important for parents to be vigilant for signs of depression as their child comes out, including: frequent sad mood, loss of interest in pleasurable activities, feelings of low self-worth, excessive guilt, hopelessness or an inability to see a happy future, thoughts of suicide, indecisiveness, inability to concentrate, agitation or restlessness, physical slowing or lethargy, overeating or loss of appetite, oversleeping or trouble sleeping and fatigue. In children and adolescents, depression often presents as increased irritability, increased restlessness and increased acting out. However, quiet, ruminative and isolative behavior can also suggest melancholic depression. Another sign of depression is an increased use or abuse of alcohol, illicit drugs and prescription drugs, such as narcotic pain medications (hydrocodone, oxycodone, codeine, etc.), methylphenidate and anxiolytics (alprazolam, lorazepam and clonazepam). Abuse of prescribed medications is a serious problem in adolescent populations. Adolescents, like adults, will sometimes reach for drugs to escape what they see as unacceptable feelings.

TALK ABOUT SAFE SEX

Gay men are at increased risk for unsafe sex, HIV and other sexually transmitted diseases. While the causes of these risks are likely multifactorial, the effect of oppression cannot be discounted. Shame and poor self-esteem detract from good decision-making, especially when it comes to sexual activity. For one thing, shame contributes to anonymous, fleeting sexual encounters in bathrooms stalls, bars, etc. When an individual believes his sexual desires are unacceptable, he or she depersonalizes sex and keeps relationships anonymous. When an individual believes his sexual feelings are dirty, he or she gives in to them rather than prepares for them. Lack of preparation and anonymity increase the risk of unsafe sex. Likewise, alcohol and drugs can numb the shame. Feelings of worthlessness add to the risk of unsafe sex. Self-worth is a prime motivator for self-care and self-preservation. Why take precautions if one has no viable future?

When your child comes out, talk to him or her about safe sex, even if s/he is college aged or you think your efforts will be met with mock gagging and rolling eyes. I'm not referring to "the birds and the bees" conversation. If you child has come out to you, s/he is beyond the basics. Have a heart-to-heart discussion about the meaning and power of sex, about intimacy and about relationships. Your conversation should connect sex with love. By putting sex in a relational context, you undo the stereotype that says homosexuality is sex stripped of meaning. You enhance feelings of relational worthiness (self-esteem). You encourage thoughtful, deliberate sexual behavior that takes into account self and other. All of these increase the likelihood of safe sex.

FAMILY ACCEPTANCE EQUALS BETTER HEALTH

Discrimination and stigmatization are associated with higher levels of stress. Higher levels of stress are associated with suicidal thoughts and drug use. LGBTQ children who view their parents as accepting of their sexual identities are less likely to cope with stress by self-destructing.[21] In a study of Latino and Caucasian LGB youths, those who reported high levels of family rejection were far more likely to attempt suicide, to use illegal drugs and to engage in unprotected sex, thus exposing themselves to sexually transmitted diseases.[22]

The connection between LGBTQ health outcomes and parental reaction to coming out is consistent and indisputable. What about the rest of the family? How does your child's coming out affect parents and siblings? Families may initially experience a family member's coming out as a loss. Grief begins with denial and moves to anger, bargaining, sadness and acceptance.[23] It might sound like this: Denial: "I don't believe it. You're not gay!" Anger: "This is going to be hard on all of us!" Bargaining: "Maybe it's a phase." Sadness: "People might hurt you or treat you badly." Acceptance: "I want to learn more about this. I want to understand."

The coming out of a child can draw a family closer as they rally in support of the gay family member. By proving loyalty and love, family ties deepen. Conversations occur that might not have otherwise taken place.

On the other hand, trust can also break down in a family when one or more family members respond poorly to a child's coming out. The worst scenario is parental rejection. Parents hold much power over self-esteem. They can also create a home environment that is so hostile that an adolescent child is compelled to live on the street. As discussed previously, street life usually leads to emotional and physical ruin. Family rejecters can also be siblings, relatives or grandparents. Though not typically as key to a child's welfare, rejection by any important family member can be a devastating blow to a child who may still be struggling with internalized homophobia. Parents need to assert to all family members that no disrespectful or abusive behavior will be tolerated in their home.

It is very important for parents to resist the natural instinct to compromise. Let's suppose that a grandparent resides with you and your gay child. Suppose the grandparent feels uncomfortable with your child's sexual orientation and asks that he not invite his "friend" to dinner. For the sake of keeping the peace, you might be tempted to ask your son if he would yield on this point. Perhaps you offer to go out to dinner, just you, your son and his partner. While this compromise may seem fair, it is not. Asking your son to accommodate prejudice implies that the grandparent's request is reasonable, thus shaming your son. The request is not reasonable. Your son should be able to bring his partner home for dinner just as he would if he were in a heterosexual relationship.

Don't ask your child to "straighten up" for another member of the family by withdrawing from events, leaving his partner out of certain family gatherings or refraining from such actions as holding his partner's hand or dancing with his partner at a wedding. Imagine that you disapproved of your heterosexual son's partner, not because the girl was disrespectful or abusive, but just because you didn't like her. Can you imagine asking your child to leave his girlfriend behind when he comes to family events? Can you imagine saying to him, "Can't you just pretend to be friends with her? Do you have to introduce her as your girlfriend?" When applied to heterosexual relationships, these requests seem rude and offensive. They are equally offensive when asked of gays.

You cannot single-handedly change the system, but you can accept your child and create a welcoming home. That alone will result in positive health effects. In addition, you can advocate for anti-bullying legislation, partner benefits (health insurance) and an end to state and federal laws that discriminate against LGBs. You can help put an end to the oppression that leads to LGB health disparities.

···

Chapter 22

Optimizing Health Care

When one segment of the population displays a greater tendency for certain health problems as compared to the general population, that group suffers from *health disparities*. When a group is identified as suffering from health disparities, the medical community tries to find out why. As discussed in previous chapters, LGBTQs suffer from a number of health disparities, e.g., they experience certain medical problems at a higher rate than the general population.

Another problem that affects LGBTQs is diminished *access to care*. There are many problems that limit access to care, such as being in a rural location or speaking a language different from that of most providers. In the case of LGBTQs, access to care has been negatively affected by lack of health insurance and the perception that healthcare providers are biased. For example, according to the Bureau of Labor Statistics, only about one-third of US employers offer same-sex partner benefits, such as health insurance. In accordance with this bias, LGBs have a greater number of unmet medical needs than their heterosexual counterparts. Lesbians are less likely than heterosexual women to receive preventive screenings such as breast exams, pap smears and mammograms. Gay men are at risk for delaying preventive screening that results in late cancer diagnosis and treatment.

While the American Medical Association recognizes that health disparities exist for LGBTQs, many medical schools and residencies still fail to provide adequate training about LGBTQ health-related concerns. In addition, many physicians feel inadequately prepared to ask their patients about sexual orientation, sexual attraction and gender orientation when taking a sexual history.[1] The lack of training affects care. Not asking about sexual and gender orientation can result in failure to screen for LGBTQ health risks, such as suicidal thinking.[2]

Many otherwise excellent physicians have not explored their internalized homophobia. Doctors who are not self-aware in this area can, by their silence or by their advice, do harm to your gay or transgender child. Because the medical interview is designed for heterosexuals, it takes special training to hear and properly respond to the needs of sexual minorities. In my experience as a health psychologist who trains physicians, only those doctors who have had this training and who have consciously explored homophobia avoid making mistakes with gay adolescents. An early bad experience with a physician can make for a later distrust of doctors and a tendency to put off health care. Studies show that gays and lesbians terminate patient-physician relationships due to perceived bias on the part of the provider.[3] Ensure that your child gets off to a good start by finding the right doctor early on.

How do you locate a gay-friendly, gay-knowledgeable physician? The Gay and Lesbian Medical Association's Web site (glma.org) has a provider directory that you can use to search for a gay-friendly physician and/or therapist. Otherwise, you can screen potential providers by asking questions such as, "Have you received any training in providing care to LGBTQs? Do you know about LGBTQ risk factors? How would they impact your management of my child's health?" If your child's physician displays an appreciation and enthusiasm for learning about LGBTQ patients, that's a good start.

Once you've found a healthcare provider, how do you know that s/he is doing a good job with your child? A physician treating LGBTQs should screen vigilantly for alcohol and drug abuse, smoking, depression and suicide. S/he should ask about bullying and be aware of the local attitudes toward gays, particularly in the school system your child attends. The physician should be able to converse comfortably about sexual orientation and sexual behavior. S/he should be able to refer you and your child to local chapters of support groups for gay youths.

Most important, your child's physician should display unconditional positive regard toward your gay child. If your child is unsure of his or her sexual orientation, the physician should maintain a neutral "wait-and-see" attitude, i.e., no push toward or against homosexuality. This neutrality is important to allow adolescents to explore their sexual thoughts and feelings freely without having to worry about being judged or prematurely labeled. If your child is transgender, the physician should also be knowledgeable about hormone reassignment or be comfortable referring your child to a specialist in sex reassignment if your child desires it.

Physicians who treat LGBTQs should also be aware of the special vulnerabilities their patients may experience during particular examinations. LGBTQs who've encountered harassment, especially in the form of physical or sexual abuse, may be afraid to expose themselves to examinations in which they are physically vulnerable, especially those examinations or procedures involving genitals or erogenous parts of the body. For lesbians and bisexual women, this includes breast and gynecological examinations; for gay and bisexual men, rectal exams and colonoscopies; for transgender individuals, those parts of the body which they hope to minimize or remove.

In addition to fear of rough treatment, LGBTQs may also feel shame during these physical exams due to internalized homophobia or, in the case of transgender people, gender dysphoria. It is not enough for physicians to treat LGBTQs the way they would anybody else during similar examinations. Physicians should carefully explore any hesitancy, offer reassurance and make their positive regard overt. These additional actions are necessary to offset the common expectation of physician bias and the increased rate of victimization in the LGBTQ population.

Heteronormative bias can make a physician visit an unpleasant experience and discourage the formation of a good patient-physician bond. Heteronormative bias is first encountered in the waiting room. Intake forms often ask whether one is "married, single or divorced." Those in gay relationships, even those with life-long partners, must check "single" or alter the form. The lack of recognition of gay relationships often continues throughout the medical interview. Physicians will automatically ask whether patients want their spouses, if they have accompanied them, present during important medical conversations. Likewise, they involve the spouse in discussions related to diet, physical activity and the patient's general function. The life partners of LGBTQs are often left out of these important conversations.

Many times lesbians have told me that, after telling their physicians about their sexual orientation, the physicians asked them if they needed birth control. Actually, physicians are trained to ask every female patient about safe sex and birth control, regardless of expressed sexual orientation, because many patients who identify as lesbian may still have sex with men. However, there are right and wrong ways to bring this up with lesbians. Ideally, the physician will say something like, "Many women who identify as lesbians still sometimes have sex with men. Is this true for you or do you exclusively have sex with women? I'm asking you this to ascertain whether there is any need to talk about birth control. Knowing about your sexual activity will also tell me if certain screenings are necessary or not."

Let's summarize the key issues that your gay, lesbian or transgender child should discuss with his or her physician. The Gay and Lesbian Medical Association's (GLMA) Web site offers lists of the things to discuss with healthcare providers for lesbians, gay men and transgender persons.[4] The information here borrows from these lists with some adaptations and additions.

LGBTQS AND THE PATIENT-PHYSICIAN RELATIONSHIP

DEPRESSION AND ANXIETY

Due to oppression and stigmatization, LGBTQs are at increased risk for developing mood and anxiety disorders. Despair can lead to suicide, even in adolescents who do not appear to be suffering from depression, especially in the early stages of coming out when internalized homophobia is not yet fully vetted. Rejection and bullying, if they occur, can make life seem unbearable. Your child needs to feel at ease talking with his or her physician, about being gay and about people's reactions when s/he discloses his or her sexual orientation. If the provider is empathic, your child will be more likely to disclose thoughts, feelings and behaviors suggestive of depression, anxiety and suicide. If needed, your physician should be able to refer your child to a culturally sensitive therapist who can offer support and help to monitor symptoms. Sometimes medications may be suggested as well.

TOBACCO

Cancers, heart disease, cerebral vascular accident (stroke) and emphysema are just four of the many potentially life-threatening consequences of smoking. Lesbians, gay men and transgender individuals are more likely to smoke than their heterosexual counterparts. Parents of gay youths should do what they can to intervene. If your child takes up smoking, explore smoking cessation options with his or her pediatrician/physician. Do this as early as possible. Smoking cessation is easier when it's addressed when the problem begins.

Why are LGBTQs so prone to smoking? There are many reasons. People often smoke as a way of managing stress and gay children, due to discrimination, experience added stress. Also, smoking is sometimes used as a means of self-medicating. Some people need a cigarette before getting out of bed each morning. Smoking can also help people self sooth. These are the folks who smoke when something upsets them. If underlying mood and anxiety disorders are detected and treated, it may reduce reliance on tobacco. Additionally, parents should work to move their LGBTQ children away from loitering in parking lots and bars and toward school-supervised activities. Parents can help by advocating for the provision of non-smoking activities that are welcoming, safe and appealing to LGBTQ youths.

ALCOHOL AND SUBSTANCE ABUSE

Just as LGBTQs are prone to smoke to deal with stress, they are also more inclined to use drugs and alcohol than their heterosexual peers. Moderate drinking (as established by the National Institute on Alcohol Abuse and Alcoholism) for healthy women is no more than three drinks per occasion and no more than a total of seven drinks per week. For healthy men, moderate drinking is no more than four drinks per occasion and no more than fourteen drinks per week. (The amount for men and women differs because gender affects how alcohol is metabolized.)

I recommend that you discourage your child from early use of alcohol, prior to the legal drinking age. This is especially important if your child has the added risk factor of having an alcoholic parent or grandparent, because genetics play a role in developing this disease. Talk to your child about alcohol before it becomes a problem and request your child's pediatrician to ask your child about alcohol use.

Much the same can be said for substance abuse and substance abuse screening. When screening for substance abuse, physicians should ask about all the common drugs such as marijuana, cocaine, heroin and methamphetamine. In addition, s/he should ask about drugs especially popular with youths, including Ecstasy (synthetic amphetamine), whippets (compressed nitrous oxide), poppers (amyl nitrite) and certain prescription drugs like narcotic pain medications.

LGBTQ youths need access to social venues that allow for dating and companionship while still offering adult supervision. LGBTQ youth groups can also provide opportunities to talk about the stress associated with being a sexual minority, which may help support self-esteem and imbue the desire for self-care. Perhaps most importantly, it is essential to keep your child in school and living at home. Once on the street, drugs and alcohol can seem the only comfort.

VERBAL AND PHYSICAL HARASSMENT

Your child's pediatrician/provider should initiate discussion about your child's school environment and ask your child directly if s/he is experiencing any verbal or physical harassment. If these things are happening, the physician should work with you to intervene on your child's behalf. If the environment proves recalcitrant to change, additional steps may be needed, such as contacting child protection services in your state.

DIET AND EXERCISE

Obesity is associated with increased risk for many serious disorders such as heart disease, cancers and diabetes. It is critical that issues related to poor diet and lack of exercise be addressed as early as possible. While some gay men struggle with obesity, others suffer from eating disorders (bulimia and anorexia nervosa). An unhealthy preoccupation with appearance can lead to the use of steroids and health supplements that can affect health adversely. Lesbians tend to have a higher body mass index than heterosexual women. As a parent, you can help your LGBTQ child develop a healthy body image by exposing him or her to healthy gay role models and a healthy, balanced lifestyle. Problems with eating disorders, which may surface in adolescence, should be addressed by a culturally competent therapist.

LESBIANS AND THE PATIENT-PHYSICIAN RELATIONSHIP

GYNECOLOGICAL EXAMINATIONS AND BREAST EXAMS

Lesbians are at a higher risk for gynecologic cancers. It is a myth that women who don't have sex with men don't need preventive screening. Many lesbians have a combination of risk factors (such as weight problems, smoking and being nulliparous or childless) that increase the chance of developing breast cancer. Add issues with gaining access to care and the result could be a delay in important medical interventions.

GAY MEN AND THE PATIENT-PHYSICIAN RELATIONSHIP

SEXUALLY TRANSMITTED DISEASES

Gay men have a high prevalence of sexually transmitted diseases (STDs). Some STDs are curable, such as syphilis, gonorrhea and chlamydia. Some are not curable, such as hepatitis A, B and C and the human papillomavirus (HPV). For years, the prevalence of HIV in the gay population was trending down, but in recent years it has been increasing. While treatment for HIV has resulted in substantial improvements in the quality and length of life of those affected, there is still no cure.

Educate your child about safe sexual practices early and often. It's the physician's job to help. S/he should be able to discuss safe sex in a knowledgeable and comfortable manner with your son. Ask your son's physician to explain his or her approach, first to you and then to your child. This allows you to evaluate the physician's knowledge and attitude before s/he gives counsel to your child and also makes it possible for your child to have a private conversation with the doctor. This will help your child make the connection between sex and relationship and will promote safe sex. Anonymous sex is often risky sex.

When vaccines are available, take advantage of them. Men who have sex with men are at increased risk of contracting hepatitis A, B and C and HPV. Hepatitis is a serious liver disease that can ultimately lead to cirrhosis and liver cancer. Vaccines are available to prevent hepatitis A and B and they are recommended for gay adolescents. There is no vaccine to prevent hepatitis C; safe sex is the only means of prevention. In addition, new evidence suggests that boys and men benefit from being immunized against HPV. The human papillomavirus can cause warts and also increases the risk of developing anal cancer. The HPV vaccine is available for both girls and boys. Most of the cancers caused by HPV affect women and for that reason, physicians are likely to advocate the strongest for the vaccination of girls. Men who have sex with men are at a higher risk for HPV-related cancers so gay male adolescents, in particular, benefit from vaccination.[5] If your child's physician does not suggest the HPV vaccine, it is a good idea to bring up the subject.

ROUTINE FOLLOW-UP

Men do not see their primary care doctors as frequently as women do. Gay men are even less likely than heterosexual men to seek preventive care. I suggest that you get your adolescent off to a good start with self-care by identifying a culturally competent pediatrician/provider. Young men need to be screened for testicular cancer and they need to be shown how to do a testicular self-exam. Gay adolescents are at risk of avoiding this examination. A positive early experience with a primary care provider will enhance trust and establish a habit of preventive screening.

TRANSGENDER PERSONS AND THE PATIENT-PHYSICIAN RELATIONSHIP

ACCESS TO HEALTH CARE

Unfortunately, sometimes when they are young (because of parental rejection), or as adults (because of employment discrimination), transgender persons are often left without health insurance and without the money to pay for health care. One of the most important things a parent can do for a transgender child is to maintain connection. This is especially true in regard to access to health care. With healthcare reform, in some instances children may remain covered by their parents' health care until the age of twenty-six.

HEALTH HISTORY

Often, transgenders do not disclose important details of their health histories to their physicians. For instance, a transgender patient might fear that disclosing a history of depression may result in failing to pass a psychological evaluation necessary for gender reassignment. Transgender patients may purposely exclude their histories of transition when visiting a new doctor, even many years after surgery. Perhaps this is due to a fear of rejection, stigmatization or negative past experiences with previous providers.

Failure to disclose important medical details can result in incomplete or inappropriate treatment. A lack of trust in a physician can also lead to dropping out of care. Parents of transgender youths can play an important role by establishing care with a pediatrician or primary care provider who is comfortable with gender identity issues, knowledgeable about transgender care and nonjudgmental toward transgender persons and those who seek gender reassignment.

HORMONES

Estrogen and antiandrogens are used in male-to-female hormonal reassignment and testosterone is used in female-to-male hormonal reassignment. Though these hormones are found in both men and women, hormone reassignment alters the balance to achieve the desired changes in secondary sexual characteristics.

Hormone therapy can have negative side effects. Estrogen can cause "blood clotting, high blood pressure, elevated blood sugar and water retention." Antiandrogens can lead to "dehydration, low blood pressure and electrolyte disturbances." Testosterone "carries the risk of liver damage." Hormone reassignment is not considered a medical need and many transgender persons will try to bypass the healthcare system to obtain treatment. It is important that hormone reassignment occur under the supervision of a physician. Parents may consider providing financial support for hormone reassignment in order to ensure medical supervision.

CARDIOVASCULAR HEALTH

Transgender persons are at increased risk for heart disease and cerebral vascular accidents (strokes) due to smoking, obesity, hormone treatment and lack of early and regular screening for hypertension and other disorders that contribute to these diseases. If a transgender male or female believes a health provider will ask him or her to stop taking hormones, the person may avoid care, even in the presence of medical symptoms. Again, it is important for parents of transgender individuals to advocate for sensitive health care. When conflicts about treatment arise, they are best handled in the context of a trusting patient-physician relationship.

CANCER

Medical checkups should include screenings for hormone-related cancer, such as breast cancer in transgender women, liver cancer in women and men and cancer of the reproductive organs in women and men. Without removal of such organs as the uterus, ovaries, breasts and prostate, transgender men and women are still at risk for developing cancer of these organs.

Some providers are uncomfortable with treating such cancers in transgender people and transgender people may avoid examinations of the parts of their bodies that they reject. As a result, these cancers may spread before detection because of a lack of preventive screening. Parents of a transgender youth need to help their child deal with the dissonance s/he may feel about obtaining preventive care when that care exposes the child to gender-based examinations that conflict with gender identity. Communicating feelings is the first step to managing them. Parental support and the support of an understanding and skilled health provider can make a big difference.

SEXUALLY TRANSMITTED DISEASES

Transgender youths who leave home are less likely to find employment and are more likely to resort to prostitution in order to survive. This puts them at high risk for HIV and other sexually transmitted diseases. Other transgender youths may put themselves at risk for unsafe sex due to discrimination, which inspires hopelessness and may lead to other types of self-destructive behavior. Furthermore, in the midst of all a transgender individual endures, concerns associated with unsafe sex may seem trivial. Parents can accentuate the importance of safe sexual practices.

ALCOHOL AND TOBACCO

Transgender people often experience rejection and depression, leading to high incidences of alcohol abuse. The introduction of sex hormones combined with alcohol abuse increases the risk of liver damage. Tobacco use is high in this group, utilized especially for suppressing appetite in an effort to lose weight. Tobacco use increases the risk of heart attacks and cerebral vascular accidents, especially when combined with administered estrogen or testosterone. If your child is transgender, talk with him or her about the increased dangers associated with combining tobacco and alcohol use with hormone reassignment. Make an arrangement to support hormone reassignment financially in exchange for your child's alcohol or tobacco moderation or abstinence. In the case of addiction, seek treatment for your child as early as possible with a culturally competent medical professional.

INJECTABLE SILICONE

Some transgender women use injectable silicone in an attempt to feminize their appearances. The silicone is often administered at "pumping parties" by non-medical persons. Silicone administered in this manner is prone to "migrate in the tissues and cause disfigurement" in the future and "is usually not medical-grade material and may contain contaminants." In addition, needle sharing has resulted in the spread of hepatitis. As your child enters adolescence, you will lose the ability to monitor his or her every action. What you can do is stay educated on the possible risks and share the information with your child so s/he can make better choices.

FITNESS (DIET AND EXERCISE)

Many transgender people work long hours to support their transitions, so exercise and healthy nutrition may not be priorities. For transgender women, exercise that promotes healthy bones and musculature may be avoided for fear of bulking up and appearing more masculine. Exercise is good for everyone and maintaining good health "prior to sex reassignment will reduce a person's operative risk and promote faster recovery." Tell your transgender child that you want him or her, above all, to stay healthy and help him or her find ways to make health a priority.

· ·
Mike's Story

Seventeen-year-old Mike was effeminate. As early as grade school, Mike began saying that he wished he were a girl. His parents were not surprised when he told them that he was transgender. After coming out, he experimented with eyeliner and mascara. Then he began discussing the idea of starting hormone therapy. His parents were anxious and frightened.

Mike has been constant in regard to his gender orientation. By taking on some of the social signals of femininity, he began to come out to the world. Coming out is different for transgender youths, because they have less control. Gays can conceal their sexual orientation to some people while being open about it with others. For instance, if a gay couple is holding hands and approaches a group of people whom they know to be aggressive toward homosexuals, they can stop holding hands and pass as heterosexuals. While this can feel cowardly, it is not. There is a time and place to take a stand and the time and the place need to be self-chosen rather than imposed by others.

Transgender individuals aren't afforded this choice. Once they take on the outward appearances of their felt genders, they take on risk. About half of all transgender individuals report experiencing physical assault due to their gender identity, with more assaults occurring to transgender females (male transitioned to female). I encouraged Mike's parents to have an open discussion with him about how people at school and in general were responding to his wearing makeup. I asked if anyone had harassed him about his gender orientation and I asked Mike to make a deal to talk with his parents right away if anyone threatened him or made him feel threatened. I also encouraged the parents to discuss Mike's gender orientation with his primary teachers, his coach, his principal, etc., to get their assurance that Mike would be treated with respect.

Mike was considering hormone therapy, which would help to align his felt gender with his appearance by increasing breast size, altering the fat-to-muscle ratio and suppressing the growth of facial hair.

Mike's gender orientation wasn't solidified, at least not to his parents. Mike had been dealing with this all his life, every day, but his parents were just coming to terms with the strength of Mike's conviction. It was natural for them to harbor the hope that Mike's gender dysphoria would vanish—that one morning he would wake up feeling like a young man and be spared the hardships of being transgender. When it becomes clear that this is not going to happen, fear can set in. Mike's parents needed to reach out for support and to talk with parents who had children at various stages of transition. Mike and his parents also needed to meet with a physician trained in providing hormone reassignment. If a well-regarded specialty center were in the area, it could offer a wide range of useful resources, including support groups for both Mike and his parents.

Besides getting the facts about transition, Mike's parents had to come to terms with losing a son and gaining a daughter. As Mike underwent hormone therapy, he began to look different and sound different from the son they raised. "She" had a new name, different from the one they'd chosen for "him." "She" had a new body, different from the one "he" was born with. In this case, parental grief should not be written off as a form of bias. While Mike's biological gender was a torment to him, it was not a torment to his parents—it was part of their beloved child's identity. Still, it was necessary for them to accept Michelle with open arms. Failure to make the shift would likely have resulted in unconscious distancing from Michelle, and that would have been the greater loss. On the other hand, letting go of Mike and joining in the transformation allowed for several benefits to emerge.

First: Transgender individuals experience their bodies as a prison. Self-disgust and hopelessness can lead to suicide. Mike's parents discovered that their melancholic son was transforming into Michelle, a hopeful, happy daughter. Happiness trumps all. Second: Though the visual changes in their child's appearance were substantial, the child was the same. If Mike loved old movies and modern art, gender transition didn't change that. If Mike was kind, funny and smart, gender transition didn't change that either. Third: Now that Mike is Michelle and no longer preoccupied by a body-soul disconnect, she will be more authentically herself with her parents. They will know the real Michelle, the one who was inside their child all along.

• •

Why spend so much time addressing health issues? How will this help you parent your gay child? It's the parents' job to educate their children as to how to lead healthy lifestyles. Parents encourage children to cover their heads in winter, to eat their vegetables and to wear their seatbelts. Now that you know more about the health risks your child may face due to oppression, discrimination and reduced access to health care, you are in a better position to advocate for prevention and to watch for indications of deteriorating health. While you could not make your child eat spinach if he pursed his lips and refused, you could play up its benefits and keep it on the table. In much the same way, you can keep health issues on the table and in the conversation when you talk to your gay child.

....
Becoming an In-Law and Grandparent

What will he look like? What will she act like? Meeting your child's partner may rekindle your homophobia. Despite your best intentions, your mind is bound to conjure up stereotypic images. If the partner turns out to fit those stereotypes, it can be unsettling, at least briefly. Once you get to know the person, stereotypes and the negative connotations attached to them wash away.

BECOMING AN IN-LAW

Social conventions, especially marriage, trigger certain behaviors in families. When a child marries, the connection between in-laws intensifies. Parents begin sending invitations to the couple and not just to their adult child. The spouse receives birthday cards and holiday presents from the in-laws. Extended family, including siblings, aunts, uncles and cousins, make similar adjustments. In some cases, fathers- and mothers-in-law from both sides of the family meet and become friends. In the happiest of circumstances, marriage affords each partner a second set of parents, a second "mom" and "dad."

Because of the social oppression that LGBTQ couples face, they may need family support even more than conventional couples do. Unfortunately, without marriage as a trigger, there is no official ritual or sacrament for LGBTQ couples that implies, "Okay, now we are family and everyone should treat us as such." It is possible for LGBTQ couples to marry in certain states and thereby obtain marriage licenses. It is also possible to marry in another country as thousands of United States citizens did in 2005 when Canada became the first country on the continent to legalize gay marriage. My spouse and I married in Massachusetts and although our marriage is not recognized in Michigan, it is recognized in some other states. Most importantly, it is recognized by us. Until marriage is legal for all, you may have to ask your child, "Are you two as good as married?" If they answer yes, welcome your child's spouse into the family.

You may want to encourage your child and his or her spouse to celebrate their union in some fashion. A state can refuse a gay couple a marriage license, but it can't stop them from having a wedding. If a wedding seems too heterosexually bound, the couple can create a ritual that feels right to them and still conveys to family and friends that a commitment has ensued. As a parent of an LGBTQ, be sure to take an interest in your child's partner's family, work, interests, etc., just as you would if they were married. Communicate that the partner is expected to attend family gatherings and that his or her presence is valued. If family rituals involve spouses, be sure that the partner is included in the same manner as the other spouses. For example, if during Hanukah each spouse lights a candle on the Menorah, be sure to involve the LGBTQ spouse in kind. The same goes for family obligations. If Thanksgiving is hosted on a rotating schedule among families, then your child and his or her partner should be expected to take a turn.

Avoid referring to the partner as your child's "friend." Their relationship is more than a friendship. Instead, ask the couple how they would like you to refer to them when introducing or discussing them.

. . . .
Emily's Story

Emily, who is twenty-four, is out as a lesbian. Emily's sister Grace was hosting Christmas dinner and her husband's side of the family is very conservative. Grace was concerned that her husband's parents would be uncomfortable if Emily came to dinner with her girlfriend. Grace asked Emily, "Can you and your girlfriend go low-key at dinner on Christmas? Maybe not hold hands or anything like that." Emily responded, "If you don't want us as we are, we're not coming. I can't believe you would even ask this of me!" Frustrated, Grace asked their parents to intervene on her behalf.

A gracious host doesn't impose conditions like this on her guests. Unfortunately, people sometimes fail to respect boundaries between family members the way they do with non-family. There is never a good reason to ask gay partners to pretend that they are straight. Doing so treats the gay relationship as second-class. More importantly, asking gays to hide their sexual orientations is asking them to shoulder feelings of shame that they may have spent years casting off. Emily's resistance to Grace's request is born of a battle with internalized homophobia. It's a healthy, hard-earned resistance that protects Emily from feeling ashamed and being shamed.

Getting in the middle of a conflict between two adult children is usually a bad idea. Conflicts between adults are always best resolved directly, in a one-on-one conversation. Grace's parents should tell her to resolve this on her own with her sister.

Sometimes, extreme reactions to homosexuality can split a family, such as when a straight person refuses to invite gay family members to events or refuses to attend events at which a gay couple is present. In these cases, everyone may feel compelled to choose sides, particularly if Christmas dinner is held at two places, one where the gay couple is welcome and one where the gay couple is not. As difficult as it may be, I encourage parents to attend only holiday events where every member of the family is welcome. Parents should make it clear that their door is always open to all of their children, regardless of sexual orientation.

•••

BECOMING A GRANDPARENT

Some people believe that there is no greater joy than becoming a grandparent. What a thrill to hold a baby, to tease out a smile, to dry a tear, to cheer every accomplishment. How satisfying to see your adult child in the role of parent, passing on the family wisdom that has trickled down through the generations. How healing, in the late years of life, to see the world through a child's innocent, imaginative eyes. You may have thought that having an LGBTQ child meant that you would never enjoy the wonders of being a grandparent. Not true!

There is no guarantee that any child, straight or gay, will want to be a parent. There are many married and unmarried heterosexuals who've chosen to remain childless. Likewise, your LGBTQ child may not be interested in parenting, but if s/he wants to parent, it can happen. More and more LGBTQ couples are choosing to raise children. The research is clear on this: children raised by gay couples fare as well or better on measures of psychological well-being when compared to children raised by heterosexual parents.[1]

When I first learned that children of gay couples, in some studies, appear better adjusted than those raised by heterosexual couples, I wondered why. Perhaps it is because gay couples don't accidently get pregnant. Because it's a choice and not an accident, they may be more prepared, emotionally and fiscally, for the responsibilities of parenting.

After recognizing that we wanted a child, my partner and I waited five years before we decided to have one. It's a good thing, too, because we needed time to work through many homophobic beliefs. We'd been telling ourselves that it was selfish to have a child, because s/he would be ostracized as the child of gay parents. We agonized over the possibility that our child might be teased. We fretted over our child not having a father. We saw ourselves, our union, as offering less to a child than that offered by a heterosexual couple.

Eventually, we realized that we had what a child needs. We loved each other; our son or daughter would grow up strong and happy under the umbrella of that love. Whatever struggles our child might face because s/he had gay parents could not outweigh the gifts we had to offer. True, we would not be able to give him or her a father, but s/he would have terrific male role models in life, especially his or her grandfather. When we finally stopped buying into the belief that our family would be inferior, we were truly ready to be parents.

It is easier for female couples to have children than male couples. As long as one of the women in the partnership is interested in bearing a child, all that is needed is a sperm donor. Frozen sperm can be purchased from sperm banks by couples or by single women. Frozen sperm is specially prepared for insemination prior to freezing. Intra-uterine and intra-cervical insemination is done by fertility clinics, many of which welcome lesbian couples. If the sperm donor is a known entity, such as a friend of the couple, there may be no need to involve a fertility clinic.

If your daughter is thinking of using a friend's semen, she should be certain that the donor has been screened for STDs. Today, there are a number of devices on the market that can help a woman pinpoint ovulation, the right time of the month to conceive. Gynecologists, primary care doctors and midwives can answer questions about the fertility cycle, prenatal counseling, and screening to promote healthy fetal development. They can also provide advice to ensure that attempts to self-inseminate are safe and efficacious. If desired, fertility specialists can also offer recommendations as to which partner, based on health status and fertility, is most likely to have a successful pregnancy. In some cases, genetic testing may be warranted to rule out the risk of certain dangerous inherited disorders.

When my partner and I decided to have a baby, we wanted to do the insemination ourselves. We looked for a guide and found none. Our sperm donor was local. He collected the semen in a small sterile cup (the kind used to collect urine samples at the doctor's office) and I rushed it home to my partner. We found that a baby medicine syringe was the best tool for insemination, and our fertility specialist recommended the proper angle of insertion. This device has a plastic flange inside the tube that collects the contents from the walls of the syringe and pushes them out so nothing is lost. Don't use the mythical turkey baster! The few teaspoons of semen the donor produces will be lost in transit.

Male same-sex couples have a more difficult time becoming parents, because someone else will have to carry their baby. It is easier and less expensive to obtain sperm from a sperm bank than it is to find donor eggs and a surrogate. State laws on the legality of paid surrogates vary and are sometimes nonexistent. Some states have formalized a legal process for use of surrogates.

Adoption and foster care are two other ways to expand a family. Some states and adoption agencies discriminate against gay couples. It will be important for your son or daughter to investigate adoption laws in his or her state. Local and state LGBTQ groups, including online groups, can be helpful. They may be able to clarify state laws regarding adoption and/or point your son or daughter to a network of LGBTQs' parents who've already negotiated this terrain. Some states and countries have created barriers that make it more difficult for gays to adopt. For some couples, having children is a top priority and may warrant moving. In all likelihood, a state or country that makes it difficult for LGBTQs to adopt may also make it difficult for gays to raise children, so moving may have multiple benefits.

Your adult son or daughter may decide against having children for any number of reasons. I can think of only one reason why you should protest: if s/he decides against having children out of a sense of inferiority or fear. If homophobia is limiting your child's life, challenge it. Be optimistic and share your optimism with your child.

Your child can be a parent and you can be a grandparent. It is more difficult for men than for women, but more male partners are adopting and utilizing surrogates. If your daughter or son believes that life without children is incomplete, encourage her or him to do whatever it takes to make it happen. Help your adult child to see the possibilities. The last thing parents want for their children is to see them settle for less or to give up. LGBTQs deserve to live fulfilling and rewarding lives and today it is within their reach.

PART V
....
THE FIGHT FOR EQUALITY

Chapter 24

Values, Rights and Laws

Values are a part of everyday life. Whether articulated or not, our values drive our aspirations and inform our decisions and opinions. What are values? The *American Heritage Dictionary* lists a number of definitions: a calculated numerical quantity; a precise meaning, as of a word; the monetary worth of something; a thing's worth as measured by its usefulness and importance; and, finally, a principle, standard, or quality considered worthwhile or desirable. Each of these definitions is interesting in its own right. There are those whose chosen values bear some of the features of all the definitions listed. Some people talk about values as if they were as concrete as a coin and as absolute as a calculation, but the last definition, the broadest one, suggests that values are actually quite abstract.

The interpretation of a value—what it means and how it translates into behavior—is complex. Religious beliefs, personal experience, culture and exposure to differing points of view are just a few of the variables that assert themselves upon a person's value system. Some political and religious groups talk about "Christian" values and "family" values, but these terms aren't clarifying. Two people who promote Christian values can differ dramatically on what they think it means to be a Christian. Is the overriding Christian value mercy or accountability, humility or righteousness? Some Christians believe in pacifism while others believe in the death penalty. Similarly, nowhere is there a list of family values to which we all agree. What one person views as a desirable value another may view with neutrality or disdain.

There are some shared, culture-based values. For instance, most United States citizens admire the ideas promoted in the Declaration of Independence, but ask them to apply those ideas to everyday life and they'll give a variety of responses.

Freedom, perhaps American citizens' most cherished value, has been a source of debate since the Declaration was written. Though Americans love freedom, it didn't come easy to them. It took the Civil War to end slavery. The right to vote, the defining freedom of a democracy, was denied to women until 1920. Why are some people so slow to stand up for freedom? The familiar is comfortable. Usually it takes a band of visionaries to help the majority see the ideal. The abolitionists and the suffragists saw the truth and they wouldn't stop fighting for these rights until everyone accepted them. Some people say that freedom isn't free. That is true. Freedom never stops growing and as it grows, it breaks boundaries. For those who value tradition and are discomforted by change, freedom comes at a cost.

· ·

Hanna's Story

Hanna, a high school student, found a mentor in Mrs. Brown, her biology teacher. Though not gay herself, Mrs. Brown supported Hanna throughout her coming out process. Hanna is now out and very happy. She started a Gay-Straight Alliance at her school and it experienced great success.

Soon Hanna began noticing that things were changing between her and her mentor. Hanna was becoming a more vocal advocate of LGBT students and pushing for change in her school. Mrs. Brown seemed increasingly weary of her efforts and had taken to telling Hanna to "slow down; these things take time." Mrs. Brown once warned Hanna that not everyone would understand or like what Hanna was doing and that she should take that into consideration.

One day, Jon, a transgender student, told Hanna that the health teacher, Mrs. Thomas, didn't say a thing about gender identity when she taught her class about sexuality. Jon said that Mrs. Thomas was unyielding when he suggested that transgender issues should be addressed when discussing LGBT issues. Hanna relayed the story to Mrs. Brown and asked her to intervene with the health teacher. Mrs. Brown refused, saying that Mrs. Thomas knew what she was doing and had the right to set her own curriculum.

In this situation, the student has surpassed the teacher. Hanna is establishing herself as a credible leader among her peers. Her confidence and leadership bode well for healthy social-emotional development. Hanna's mentor may not have the courage or the will to challenge the system. She may be a more careful person or someone who is uncomfortable with conflict. To her credit, Mrs. Brown has contributed significantly to Hanna's self-esteem, but she has taken Hanna as far as she can. Hanna now needs to look for mentors among those who have experience in leadership. It would be ideal if she could connect with people at the state level of student organizations. This would give her a chance see how gay rights are achieved in schools in other locales, schools both more and less progressive than her own. Hanna will meet obstacles and she will upset some people. Many people in addition to Mrs. Brown will tell her, "Slow down. You can't expect people to understand. You can't expect people to accept this!" Hanna must persevere for what she perceives as right.

In the gay community it is often said, "Silence will not protect you." While the converse of this is not always true at the individual level, it is wholly true for the gay community at large: "Speaking out will make you safe."

•••

How you react to your gay child and how your family as a whole reacts is irrevocably tied to values. Ask yourself: *What does freedom mean to me?* Now that you have a gay child, you're likely to find yourself thinking about freedom in new ways or at least from a new perspective. This may prompt you to examine other values, such as those associated with heterosexuality, parenting and social behaviors. To maintain and strengthen your relationship with your child, you have to be open to discussing values, especially when values conflict.

Conflict is not always a bad thing; it is the natural result of applying values to real-life situations. When dearly held values conflict, which they will, it tests a person's convictions and deepens his or her insight. Perhaps you find yourself facing conflicting values. For instance, you may have thought of yourself as committed to family values. Your working definition of family values included both putting family first and maintaining a stance against homosexuality. Maybe you cherish your faith but now find its stance against your child's sexual orientation untenable. Now your son or daughter has come out as gay and you have to decide which of those ideas, family first or anti-gay, is the priority. You may find yourself reflecting and examining all your assumptions about family values.

I am not suggesting that you adopt a new set of values for the sake of smoothing out a potential conflict with your gay child. Rather, I am encouraging you to take advantage of the opportunity engendered by your child's coming out. If you have never seriously discussed your views on homosexuality with LGBTQs, do so now. If you've never thought about gay rights, read and think about them now. Some say faith is not faith unless it is tested. The same can be said for values. Building a bridge between yourself and your child may result in surprising personal growth.

Chapter 25

Marriage Matters

The right to love, to declare that love and to have that declaration acknowledged is the epitome of what it means when we talk about *inalienable* human rights. Marriage holds the family together. It transforms the hope of a lasting love into the promise of a lasting family. It is a piece of evidence of a couple's commitment. Without legalized marriage, gay rights will always fall short of human rights. Calling gay unions "civil unions" and not marriage opens the door to challenges regarding every aspect of gay rights. Civil unions are no substitute for marriage. Separate rights are never equal rights.

There is another reason why parents of gay children need to think about marriage. It will be impossible to understand your child's experience growing up gay without appreciating the relevance of the culture war over marriage. Never before have gays been so visible, let alone the object of constant political rhetoric. This exposes your child to a great deal of stimuli, some of which are heart wrenching and some of which are heart lifting. The debate and the outcome will impact your child's life. If your state is considering legislation for or against gay marriage, talk about it with your child. Ask her what she's heard. Ask him how he feels. Your child will need your support if the marriage war comes to your state and puts him or her on the front lines.

THE STATE OF GAY MARRIAGE TODAY

There has been an increase of about 52 percent in the number of same-sex households since 2001.[1] Between 2004, when Massachusetts became the first state to legalize gay marriage, and 2010, about fifty thousand gay couples have married.[2] The available data from the United States Census in 2010 indicates that there were 594,000 same-sex couple households, about 1 percent of the US population. In states that had legalized gay marriage, about 42 percent of same-sex couple households identified as married compared with about 28 percent for states with domestic partnerships or civil unions and about 23 percent for all other states.[3]

Attitudes are changing. According to the Pew Research Center, the American public is moving steadily toward a growing acceptance of gay marriage; Pew reports that 46 percent of Americans favor gay marriage, 44 percent are against it and the remainder are unsure. The number of those in favor of gay marriage is steadily rising. Though younger Americans are most inclined to favor gay marriage, older minds are being swayed as well, albeit at a lower incline. Attitudes toward gay marriage also vary by race and religion. About 50 percent of whites support gay marriage, compared to 39 percent of non-whites. Among religions, the greatest opposition comes from white Evangelical Protestants, followed by black Protestants.[4]

CURRENT STATUS OF MARRIAGE LAW

A number of countries have recognized the need for equality in marriage. Same-sex marriage has been legalized in the Netherlands, Belgium, Spain, Canada, South Africa, Norway, Sweden, Portugal, Denmark, Iceland and Argentina. Legislation to allow same-sex marriage is pending in the United Kingdom, Nepal, Luxembourg, Finland and Uruguay.

Here in the United States, only eight states—Massachusetts, Vermont, Connecticut, Iowa, New Hampshire, New York, Maryland and Washington state—and the District of Columbia have legalized same-sex marriage. In June of 2008, the California Supreme Court ruled in favor of same-sex marriage, but the right was rescinded just months later when voters passed Proposition 8, amending the state constitution to restrict marriage to a man and a woman. While Rhode Island does not convey marriage licenses to same-sex couples, it does honor the marriage licenses of same-sex couples legally obtained in other states.

Civil unions appear to be more acceptable to many Americans. Seven states offer civil unions that are legally equivalent to marriage: California, Delaware, Hawaii, Illinois, New Jersey, Nevada and Oregon. Three additional states, Colorado, Maine and Wisconsin, have passed laws that provide same-sex couples with some, but not all, of the entitlements of marriage.

Thirty states have amended their constitutions to limit marriage to a man and a woman. These states, along with the year that the amendment was passed, are: Alabama (2006), Alaska (1998), Arizona (2008), Arkansas (2004), California (2008), Colorado (2006), Florida (2008), Georgia (2004), Idaho (2006), Kansas (2005), Kentucky (2004), Louisiana (2004), Michigan (2004), Mississippi (2004), Missouri (2004), Montana (2004), Nebraska (2000), Nevada (2002), North Carolina (2012), North Dakota (2004), Ohio (2004), Oklahoma (2004), Oregon (2004), South Carolina (2006), South Dakota (2006), Tennessee (2006), Texas (2005), Utah (2004), Virginia (2006) and Wisconsin (2006).

A small group of states, including the state where I live, took the attack on gay marriage one step further. These states enacted laws or amendments that could be interpreted (and, in some cases, have been interpreted) to restrict the recognition of same-sex unions beyond that of denying marriage. The states are: Alabama, Arkansas, Florida, Georgia, Kentucky, Idaho, Louisiana, Michigan, Nebraska, North Carolina, North Dakota, Ohio, Oklahoma, South Carolina, South Dakota, Texas, Utah, Virginia and Wisconsin.

For instance, the state I live in, Michigan, passed a constitutional amendment in 2004 that restricts marriage to a man and a woman. Beyond that, the amendment bans the recognition of any same-sex union for "any purpose." Since its passage, city governments that had been offering partner benefits to their employees are now prohibited from continuing to do so. After threatening to sue the state, the University of Michigan was exempted from having to comply. The University successfully argued that losing partner benefits made it less attractive to prospective faculty.

Another impact of the amendment was to restrict second parent adoption to married couples. My wife is the biological parent of our child. Though I am emotionally and fiscally his parent and have been since his birth, I am denied the right to adopt him. This hurts our son as much as it does us. He cannot benefit from my health insurance or from any other benefit tied to adoption. In addition, I have no rights related to his health care. For example, if our son has a medical emergency and my spouse is not present, I would need to produce a signed consent statement from her that has been updated within the past six months in order to make medical decisions on our son's behalf. In some states, I could even be denied the right to visit him in the hospital. Laws like these fly in the face of truth and rationality, revealing themselves to be what they are: perversions of justice and assaults on freedom.

LEGAL BENEFITS OF MARRIAGE

The Human Rights Campaign (HRC) is the largest LGBTQ advocacy organization in the United States and an excellent resource for state and national data on all legal issues that affect LGBTQs. According to the HRC, there are more than one thousand legal rights associated with marriage that are denied to gay couples. Access to health care is just the beginning. For example, gay individuals cannot leave their pensions or social security benefits to their partners. They have to hire lawyers to establish protections related to finances and home ownership that married couples enjoy without hassle. Gay couples are not entitled to the benefits of the Family Leave Act. If a partner is hospitalized, the other can be denied visitation. Gays can be left out of decision-making regarding partners' medical care. They are denied many tax benefits. They are not entitled to the same work-related visa opportunities as married couples.

There are also many less obvious benefits of marriage that are frequently denied to gay partners. Spouses are invited to graduations, award dinners and orientations. They are acknowledged in speeches that laud the achievements of their partners. When a soldier dies, his or her spouse is given the flag in recognition of the loss. Spouses are compensated in the case of tragedy, such as the monetary support offered by the government and charities to the spouses of the victims of September 11. Spouses are the topic of informal but important conversations. Small disclosures about family and spouses create personal connections that smooth the path of professional relations. In some cases, spouses are expected to stand up for their wives or husbands in a display of family pride, as politicians do when campaigning.

MARRIAGE LAWS AND THEIR EFFECT ON LGB HEALTH AND WELL-BEING

In a thorough review of the effects of marriage on health, Dr. Robert G. Wood, Dr. Brian Goesling and Dr. Sarah Avellar of Mathematica Policy Research identified marital benefits related to healthcare access, mental health and effects on children. They found that married people have better access to private health insurance and receive care in higher-quality hospitals. Men and women in stable marriages have fewer depressive symptoms and smaller increases in depressive symptoms over time as compared to men and women in stable unmarried relationships. In addition, entry into a first marriage is associated with a decline in alcohol and marijuana use in young adults. Children who grow up in two-parent families live longer and enjoy better adult health than children from single-parent families.[5] While these results are likely based primarily on heterosexual marriages, there is little reason to think that gay marriage would not confer similar benefits. I strongly suspect that the psychological benefit of marriage for gay couples surpasses that of heterosexual couples due to its de-stigmatizing effect.

Conversely, anti-gay marriage amendments and the campaigns associated with them have taken a toll on the health and well-being of gays and lesbians and their children by turning them into second-class citizens in the eyes of the law.[6] Psychologist Dr. Sharon Scales, along with Dr. Ellen Riggle, Dr. Sharon Horne and Dr. Angela Miller, found higher levels of stress, depressive symptoms and negative affect among LGBs who lived in the nine states that passed anti-gay marriage amendments during the 2006 election when compared with LGBs from states who did not pass such amendments. The psychological distress was attributed to exposure to negative media messages, negative conversations and feelings about the passage of the amendment.[7]

When my state passed its anti-gay marriage amendment, I was devastated. My feelings ran the gamut from disbelief to rage to despair. I could not accept the fact that people were voting on something as personal as whom I married. As I walked around the streets of my town and down the halls of my workplace, I wondered which people might have voted against my rights. I felt alienated from my state and even from those around me who had occupied a seat of power over my freedom. Before the law was passed, I could rationalize away some of the stress I experienced when I heard negative chatter about gays. I could tell myself that the people I knew didn't think that way. After the law passed, it was harder to do so. The slander I heard almost daily on the TV and radio regarding the passage of the amendment robbed me of considerable mental resources for some time. As a direct consequence of this experience, I began writing about gay rights.

....
Legal Protections

Suze Orman, the well-known financial advisor, stated on *The View*, "My social issue affects my financial issue. And the reason why it affects my financial issue is that if I die, Kathy—my partner—is going to lose 50 percent of what I have because we can't be married."

Survey your state or national statutes relevant to LGBTQs. The Human Rights Campaign Web site has information in a number of accessible and understandable formats. If you explore the laws, you'll discover that a wide range of regulations impact LGBTQs. One key law you'll want to know about: Does the state in which your daughter or son lives prevent employers from firing based on sexual orientation? The majority of states do not offer such protection, leaving LGBTQs victim to the biases of their employers. On the other hand, towns, cities and individual employers sometimes provide such protection in the absence of state law. My employer includes LGBTQs in its documented commitment to nondiscrimination in hiring and firing, even though the State of Michigan offers no such protection. It is important that your daughter or son know if s/he is afforded employment protection from at least one of these entities. I would be hesitant to sign an employment contract without it.

Advocate to change employment biases and, until this happens, advise your son or daughter to protect him or herself in the absence of employment or housing rights by avoiding locales that allow discrimination. There is quite a bit your child can and should do to protect his or her rights regarding a relationship. If your child has a life partner whom s/he cannot marry, both partners will need to complete some important paperwork. While it is best for your child and the partner to see an attorney who specializes in such matters, I offer some suggestions:

Each partner should meet with his or her primary care provider (PCP) to complete a document called a Medical Durable Power of Attorney. This form may have a different title in your state, but your child's PCP will be well acquainted with the state's version and have copies in the office. The Medical Durable Power of Attorney tells the PCP and hospital providers what types of treatment the patient prefers and does not prefer in the event of a medical crisis, if the patient is unable to make decisions for him or herself. It allows the patient to state whom s/he chooses to make these decisions instead.

Incompetence is a temporary mental state. Be aware that people are incompetent for certain decisions at certain times. A patient who is unconscious cannot make any decisions. One who has a mild brain injury is competent for some decisions but not necessarily for all decisions. If the patient is deemed unable to care for him or herself and this condition is expected to be long lasting or permanent, then the court appoints a legal guardian. A legal guardian will sometimes have the authority to make many types of decisions for the patient, including financial and medical decisions, but, if desired, these responsibilities can be divided among different individuals. No one wants to think that a loved one will suffer a major medical crisis, but it does happen. Encourage your adult child to get his or her wishes in writing and to do so long before s/he thinks is necessary. If your child's life situation changes, s/he can always reverse or alter legal paperwork.

Married couples are bound financially as well as emotionally. Unmarried couples need to ensure this is understood by government, banks and other financial institutions. Make sure that partners hold bank accounts jointly. In the event that one partner becomes ill or dies, the money will still be accessible by the other partner. Likewise, all property should be jointly held: vehicles, homes, rental properties and land. Your child and his or her partner need to write wills, even though they are young and healthy. Failure to do so will result in a lack of recognition of a partner's rights to property, even property to which s/he has financially contributed but is not listed as part owner. If your child wants his or her belongings to be passed on to a partner, s/he needs to indicate this in a will.

When state laws prohibit gay marriage and second parent adoption, intentions about children should be made clear in a written document. Imagine that your daughter's partner bears a child whom they raise together. If the partner, the biological mother of your grandchild, dies before creating a will, your daughter will have no parental rights. If the partner's parents were hostile toward your daughter and/or their daughter's lifestyle, they could take custody of your grandchild, leaving you and your daughter with no legal recourse. Even when family members get along well, it is better to be sure there is no reason that courts can delay or object to your daughter's parental rights. A will prevents such disasters.

Your child needs to talk with his or her employer or the employer's human resources department about benefits. If the employer does not offer the full range of partner benefits, the employer still may allow your child to select the primary beneficiary for some benefits such as life insurance or a one-time death benefit. Roth, 401(k), 403(b) and IRA accounts allow for an intended beneficiary, which need not be a spouse. Many employers allow employees to opt in for additional life insurance for little extra cost; this is well worth considering for gay couples who, in most states, don't inherent spousal social security and pension benefits. If a pension benefit, distributed monthly, does not transfer to an unmarried partner, your child might consider taking his or her pension in a lump sum so s/he can transfer the funds to an IRA and list a partner as the beneficiary and a child (the partner's biological son or daughter) as the co-beneficiary or contingent beneficiary.

Divorce is another matter that could be a problem. In the case of marriage, the court divides property and other assets. Unmarried gay couples, especially those without civil unions, don't have access to the courts. Like most splitting couples, they may have strong feelings about who should have what. Your child and his or her partner should include among their legal documents agreements related to property in case of separation. One option is to agree to have a legal arbitrator or mediator handle the division of assets.

All couples want to grow old together, in peace. Some assisted living facilities and nursing homes accommodate gay couples. Your son or daughter should explore these institutions and make his or her wishes clear to children and other family members. It is tragic when a loving couple is denied sharing a room due to an antiquated nursing home rule.

Additionally, gay couples need to talk about other end-of-life issues: whether they want to donate organs, leave their bodies to a medical school, be cremated or be buried together. These wishes need to be clear ahead of time.

Until marriage is completely available to gay couples, they will need to patch together these legal protections to ensure that their wishes are honored.

....
Positively Gay

To be happy, a person has to love him or herself. If shame is not jettisoned at liftoff, it will be hard for your child to leave the ground, let alone soar. When gays accept their sexual orientations and reject negative beliefs about homosexuality, they have every chance for happiness. Journalist Andrew Sullivan states in *The Daily Beast*, "And as I experienced intimacy and love for the first time as an adult, all that brittleness of the gay adolescent, all that white-knuckled embarrassment, all those ruses and excuses and dark, deep depressions lifted. Yes, this was happiness."[1]

A study by Suffolk University psychology professor Dr. Jane A. Bybee and her contemporaries compared gay and heterosexual men at two age points (eighteen to twenty-four and twenty-five to forty-eight) and found that gay men twenty-five and older showed fewer mental health problems on measures of depression, suicidality, anger, negative self-esteem, emotional instability and emotional unresponsiveness as compared to younger gay men. Decreases in chronic shame accounted, in part, for the age-related decreases in depression. In fact, the mental health of gay and heterosexual men over twenty-five years of age appeared quite similar, particularly among men who were out and accepting of their sexual orientations.[2] Similarly, psychologists Dr. Anthony D'Augelli and Dr. Arnold Grossman found that lower internalized homophobia in older LGBs was associated with a lower lifetime prevalence of suicidal thinking and less loneliness.[3]

Unfortunately, the majority of studies conducted on the LGBTQ population focus on minority stress and the toll it takes on the health of gays and lesbians. There is only a smattering of studies that explore the positive aspects of being gay. As discussed earlier, University of Akron researchers Michelle Vaughan and Charles Waehler discovered "coming out growth"—strengths spawned from dumping homophobia and integrating sexual orientation; strengths that enhanced successful navigation through the broader scope of social-developmental tasks.

Dr. Ellen Riggle, professor at the University of Kentucky, and several of her peers asked over five hundred gays and lesbians from forty-five states how positive they felt about being gay or lesbian. Ninety percent of respondents said they felt "extremely positive" or "very positive," 8.5 percent were "somewhat positive" and only 1 percent were "not very positive" or "not at all positive." The researchers also asked participants what they thought was positive about being gay. The many responses received can be grouped into three themes:[4]

- **Gays and lesbians felt that being gay made them more sensitive to oppression and more empathic toward those who are discriminated against for any reason.**

    Not everyone who is exposed to oppression becomes more empathic. The frequent mention of this among gays and lesbians in this study is interesting and worth more investigation. In this study, many of the participants were able to connect unfairness done to them with unfairness done to others. Respondents said that being gay gave them a deeper, richer insight into the nuances of discrimination. There was courage gained in having shrugged off mainstream expectations, enabling a greater willingness to advocate for those being discriminated against, as well as a general comfort in speaking up. Empathy appeared to be enhanced by hard-earned authenticity. Having searched one's soul to discover the true self, gays and lesbians reported feeling present in their relationships with others, thus enhancing the empathic connection.

- **Gays and lesbians thought that being gay freed them from social constraints that might otherwise limit them, particularly in regard to gender roles, but in a broader sense as well.**

     Parting with sexual norms allowed the gays and lesbians in this study to examine a wide variety of social constraints and to decide, for themselves, if particular rules and values truly resonated with their beliefs. They talked about exploring gender roles, communication and division of power in their relationships. They perceived themselves as having greater liberty to be creative in how they conceived relationships and in how they problem solved. Lesbians often commented that there was greater equity in their relationships with women, compared to past relationships with men. Gay men found that they could be more disclosing of feelings and vulnerabilities to partners and friends, without fear of being seen as weak. In fact, gay men said that heterosexual men were more inclined to disclose to them than to heterosexual friends. Perhaps the heterosexual men perceived the gay men as more empathic and less judgmental in regard to gender expectations related to expression of feelings.

- **Gays and lesbians thought that being gay offered them access to a community of friends who were steadfast and understanding.**

     This was more than having access to a community of like-minded people. The diversity within the gay community was considered a strength. Gays and lesbians expressed a high degree of devotion to caring for other gays and lesbians. This devotion may stem, in part, from being shunned by families of origin. In that void, gays and lesbians began a tradition of embracing one another like sisters and brothers. Anyone immersed in the community knows that many gays create chosen families, the bonds of which are as strong as any traditional family. These families tackle day-to-day tasks, celebrate holidays and nurse each other in sickness. Gays who have suffered abandonment by their families of origin cherish the ties of chosen families. They can display heroic loyalty and an intractable sense of duty.

Interestingly, many participants reported that being gay also enhanced their connections with heterosexuals. As noted, the gay men thought it led to deeper relationships with heterosexual men, but they also said that it opened the door to abiding friendships with heterosexual women as well. Eliminating the possibility of romantic engagement allowed them to have close platonic relationships with women, even married women. Likewise, lesbians felt that heterosexual women were not put off by their sexual orientation and heterosexual men could become close friends with them without worrying about that closeness being misperceived as a desire for romantic attachment.

In the early stages of coming out, I was possessed by what I had to lose. I thought being gay meant having a harder and less fulfilling life. I thought being gay could prove to be disastrous. The truth was I was thrust forward by a feeling and into a life that I could not imagine. Now I feel differently. Like the gays and lesbians in Riggle's study, I associate being gay with gains in personal growth. My story turned out differently than I expected, but, in many ways, better than I could have dreamed.

············
Conclusion

Every gay soul knows a thousand blows. This can leave the soul soft and flexible or tough and scarred. The difference is in the healing and in the hoping. Teach your child resiliency: how to bend without breaking, how to move through patches of difficulty without getting stuck in them. With resiliency, no wound is beyond healing. Teach your child hope. Be like the light at the end of the tunnel, the reminder that there is a way out and an end to suffering. Things are getting better for LGBTQs every day. There is every reason to believe that your son or daughter will have a bright future, even if the present seems fraught with difficulty.

LGBs are now out in the world. With increased exposure, there has been a decrease in homophobia. "Don't ask, don't tell" has ended and LGBs now serve openly in the military. According to most polls, many people around the world think civil unions should be legalized and gay marriage appears to be picking up traction with less negative reaction. LGBs, I believe, will never again suffer the oblivion of invisibility. They are out and they are staying out.

Unfortunately, a lot of transgender individuals struggle for acceptance. I believe that the forward movement in LGB rights can only help to bring discrimination against transgender individuals to the forefront. The increased focus on school bullying is also helping to advance transgender issues as evidenced by the inclusion of transgender victims in federal hate crime legislation.

Here's what this is all about: Your child walking freely about in the middle of the day, under the brightest sun, feeling great about who he or she is and excited about who he or she hopes to become. It's about freedom for your child to be the same person whether alone or in a crowded room. It's about the freedom to love. Your child deserves the real thing: a lasting, resilient love. A love that refuses to be confined to a small, dark corner. It is never only about sex. The desire for sex can be satisfied easily enough, without facing all the difficulties of coming out. One major reason your child has made this announcement about sexual orientation is because he or she desires a loving relationship. The only thing worth all this trouble is love.

Don't let your child settle for less. When your son or daughter talks to you about being gay, don't get stuck on the sex. Sex can be an expression of love, but it is not love. Focus on love and remind your child that the desire for a lasting intimate relationship is a healthy desire. Believe in love and encourage your child to believe in it too.

This book has been about two kinds of love. The first is love in the context of gay relationships. The second is love in the context of the parent-child relationship. Both are natural, healthy forms of love and so both are imbued with all of the wonderful characteristics of love: patience, tolerance, fidelity, kindness, and courage. Your child has followed love's lead by coming out despite discrimination and homophobia. Now it's your turn to follow love's lead and come around.

LGBTQ RESOURCES

RECOMMENDED WEB SITES

AMPLIFY

Provides information for LGBTQ children and teens on how to become activists in their schools and communities.

www.amplifyyourvoice.com

CAMP PRIDE

Conducts a five-day leadership camp for LBGT individuals ages eighteen and older, held at Vanderbilt University. Participants explore LGBT issues on personal and national levels. Its mission is to increase individual and community pride and awareness and to develop leadership skills in those planning to pursue roles as leaders of change.

www.campuspride.org/camppride/index.html

EYES ON BULLYING

"Offers a multimedia program to prepare parents and caregivers to prevent bullying in children's lives. Features the Eyes on Bullying Toolkit with insights, strategies, skills-building activities, and resources."

www.eyesonbullying.org

FENWAY HEALTH

Located in the Boston area, Fenway Health is dedicated to providing optimal health care for LGBTQs. Their resource page is excellent.

www.fenwayhealth.org/site/PageServer?pagename=FCHC_res
_resources_home

GAY FAMILY SUPPORT

Suited for parents, this Web site is written by the mother of one gay son and one bisexual son. It's a mother's story of how her family adjusted to their children coming out, with an inside look at the gay community and how you and your child can connect with that great network of support. Information on the language of the gay culture, FAQs, book recommendations, parents' stories and a gay pride store provide a casual welcome into this community.

www.gayfamilysupport.com

GAY AND LESBIAN ALLIANCE AGAINST DEFAMATION (GLAAD)

Provides advocacy and holds the media accountable for the image it presents to the public about the gay community. It also promotes a true understanding of LGBT lives. Its goal is to increase awareness, thereby decreasing the stigma, stereotyping and marginalization of those within the LGBT community.

www.glaad.org

GAY AND LESBIAN MEDICAL ASSOCIATION (GLMA)

Created by physicians and other healthcare providers, GLMA is interested in improving health care for LGBTs through advocacy and education. Their Web site provides reliable, evidenced-based information on LGBT health. It also offers a gay-friendly provider directory.

www.glma.org

GAY, LESBIAN & STRAIGHT EDUCATION NETWORK (GLSEN)

Devoted to change, GLSEN works with students, schools, parents and the community to ensure that students in the LGBT community are safe in their school environments and respected for their differences. They provide training and support on the national and local levels for educators, principals, district leaders and government leaders who work toward building school cultures that embrace the differences of their LGBT students.

www.glsen.org

GLBT NATIONAL HELP CENTER

Provides peer counseling online and by phone to members of the LGBT community, information on national and local resources, FAQs, a blog and a Youth Talkline for those under twenty-five years of age.

www.glnh.org

HUMAN RIGHTS CAMPAIGN (HRC)

Committed to justice, the HRC is the largest LGBT civil rights advocacy organization. They operate at both a grassroots level and nationally. The site offers a trove of information on LGBT legal rights at the state and national levels. Their popular logo, a yellow equal sign with a dark blue background, conveys the organization's mission: to achieve equal rights for LGBTs.

www.hrc.org

IT GETS BETTER

Started by Dan Savage, It Gets Better is a place for young LGBT individuals and those who love them who may be wondering what the future holds. Inspirational videos, blogs and a list of over 500,000 people taking a pledge to end bigotry against those within the LGBT community can be viewed on this site.

www.itgetsbetter.org

LAMBDA LEGAL

Advocates in the courts for gay rights and serves as a legal resource for gays and lesbians.

www.lambdalegal.org

METROPOLITAN COMMUNITY CHURCH

Established in 1968, The Metropolitan Community Church was the first church with an affirming ministry toward the LGBT community. Today they have a worldwide ministry with churches around the globe.

www.mccchurch.org

MY RIGHT SELF

Offers information on gender transitioning, personal stories and links to other useful sites.

www.myrightself.org

NATIONAL BULLYING PREVENTION CENTER

Assists adults who want to learn how to stop school bullying, with a focus on protecting children with disabilities and elementary school children. Also offers information on Bullying Prevention Awareness Week.

www.pacer.org/bullying/

NATIONAL GAY AND LESBIAN TASK FORCE

Trains activists, organizes gay rights campaigns and advances pro-LGBT legislation. See this Web site for cutting-edge information.

www.thetaskforce.org

NATIONAL VIOLENCE PREVENTION YOUTH RESOURCE CENTER

Offers information and links to assist parents, teachers and teenagers with preventing bullying.

www.safeyouth.org

PARENTS, FAMILIES AND FRIENDS OF LESBIANS AND GAYS (PFLAG)

Dedicated to realizing the dream of full inclusion of the LGBT community in mainstream society. There are currently over 500 local chapters providing opportunities for emotional support and empowerment. You can locate a chapter through the Web site. If there is no chapter near you, PFLAG will provide the information you need to start one. In addition, the site offers information on education, activism, legal and employment matters, civil rights and resource links for LGBT citizens and their friends and families.

www.pflag.org

THE POINT FOUNDATION

Provides scholarships, mentorship and internship opportunities for students pursuing higher education. Students accepted into the program are matched with professionals in their fields of interest. These mentors provide support and advice throughout the students' college tenures.

www.pointfoundation.org

STOPBULLYING.GOV

Managed by the Department of Health and Human Services, this site helps children, young adults, parents and educators put an end to bullying.

www.stopbullying.gov

THE TREVOR PROJECT

Provides crisis intervention and suicide prevention to LGBTQ youths.

www.thetrevorproject.org

RECOMMENDED BOOKS

Fenway Guide to Lesbian, Gay, Bisexual, and Transgender Health edited by Harvey J. Makadon, Kenneth H. Mayer, Jennifer Potter and Hilary Goldhammer (American College of Physicians, 2007)

Gay America: Struggle for Equality by Linas Alsenas (Amulet Books, 2008)

Love Undetectable by Andrew Sullivan (Vintage, 1998)

The Meaning of Matthew by Judy Shepard (Hudson Street Press, 2009)

Meeting Jesus Again for the First Time: The Historical Jesus and the Heart of Contemporary Faith by Marcus J. Borg (HarperOne, 1995)

The New Jewish Wedding, Revised by Anita Diamant (Scribner, 2001)

Protection Portfolio by Suze Orman (Hay House, 2002)

Queer America: A People's GLBT History of the United States by Vicki L. Eaklor (The New Press, 2011)

What the Bible Really Says About Homosexuality by Daniel A. Helminiak (Alamo Square Press, 2000)

RECOMMENDED MOVIES

Angels in America (HBO Home Video, 2003)
Big Eden (Wolfe Video, 2000)
Boys Don't Cry (Fox Searchlight Pictures, 1999)
Brokeback Mountain (Universal, 2005)
But I'm a Cheerleader (Lionsgate, 1999)
Chutney Popcorn (Wolfe Video, 2000)
For the Bible Tells Me So (First Run Features, 2007)
If These Walls Could Talk (HBO NYC Productions, 1996)
A Jihad for Love (First Run Features, 2007)
Philadelphia (Sony Pictures Home Entertainment, 1993)
Trembling Before G-d (New Yorker Films, 2001)

GAY SYMBOLS AND THEIR MEANINGS

THE RAINBOW FLAG

The diverse colors in the rainbow have come to symbolize the diversity of sexual orientation and gender.

THE PINK TRIANGLE

Now used as a symbol of solidarity, its origins stem back to the Nazi concentration camps. Among Hitler's victims were gays and lesbians. Instead of wearing the Jewish star, they were made to wear a pink triangle.

♀♀ AND ♂♂

Symbols that represent two women or two men in a relationship.

The equal sign is the logo of The Human Rights Campaign (HRC). It is yellow on a dark blue background.

PART I: TEMPERING FIRST REACTIONS

CHAPTER 3: FIRST REACTIONS

1 Kinsey, Pomeroy and Martin, *Sexual Behavior in the Human Male*; Kinsey, Pomeroy, Martin and Gebhard, *Sexual Behavior in the Human Female*

2 Haas et al., "Suicide and Suicide Risk in Lesbian, Gay, Bisexual, and Transgender Populations."

CHAPTER 4: WHAT NOT TO SAY

1 Masters, Johnson and Kolodny, *Masters and Johnson on Sex and Human Loving*.

CHAPTER 6: GETTING IT RIGHT WHEN YOU CAN'T AGREE

1 Jonathan Capehart, "'Hoax' Against Hate Crimes Bill," *Washington Post*, April 30, 2009, http://voices.washingtonpost.com/postpartisan/2009/04/hoax_against_hate_crimes_bill.html.

CHAPTER 7: PARENTAL ADJUSTMENTS

1 Wilson, Zeng and Blackburn, "An Examination of Parental Attachments."

2 Padilla, Crisp and Rew, "Parental Acceptance and Illegal Drug Use."

3 Ryan et al., "Family Rejection as a Predictor of Negative Health Outcomes."

4 Bowes et al., "Families Promote Emotional and Behavioral Resilience to Bullying."

5 Muller, *Parents Matter.*

6 Potoczniak, Crosbie-Burnett and Saltzburg, "Experiences Regarding Coming Out to Parents"; Saltzburg, "Parents' Experience of Feeling Socially Supported."

7 Ray, *Lesbian, Gay, Bisexual and Transgender Youth*

8 Saltzburg, "Parents' Experience of Feeling Socially Supported."

9 Beeler and DiProva, "Family Adjustment Following Disclosure of Homosexuality by a Member."

PART II: HOMOPHOBIA

CHAPTER 8: UNDERSTANDING HOMOPHOBIA

1 Wilkinson's, "Religiosity, Authoritarianism, and Homophobia," 58.

2 Schwartz, "With or Against Us"; Herek and Garnets, "Sexual Orientation and Mental Health."

3 Schwartz, "With or Against Us"; Finlay and Walther, "The Relation of Religious Affiliation."

4 Newman, "Lesbians, Gays, and Religion."

5 Schwartz, "With or Against Us."

6 Herek and Capitanio, "'Some of My Best Friends'."

7 Schiappa, Gregg and Hewes, "Can One TV Show Make a Difference?"

8 Newcomb and Mustanski, "Internalized Homophobia and Internalizing Mental Health Problems."

9 Frost, "Internalized Homophobia and Relationship Quality."

CHAPTER 9: DISSECTING STEREOTYPES

1 Jesse Hamlin, "Quotes from Harvey Milk and friends," *San Francisco Chronicle*, November 23, 2008, www.sfgate.com/cgi-bin/article.cgi?f=/c/a/2008/11/21/PKBJ13VKO5.DTL.

2 Ashmore and Del Boca, "Conceptual Approaches to Stereotypes and Stereotyping," 16.

3 Brown and Groscup, "Homophobia and Acceptance of Stereotypes."

4 Savin-Williams, *The New Gay Teenager.*

5 Fagan et al., "Pedophilia."

CHAPTER 11: WHEN HOMOPHOBIA MORPHS INTO HATE

1 Herek, Gillis and Cogan, "Psychological Sequelae of Hate Crime Victimization."

2 Adams, Wright and Lohr, "Is Homophobia Associated with Homosexual Arousal?"

3 Walker and Bright, "False Inflated Self-Esteem and Violence."

CHAPTER 12: RELIGION AND HOMOPHOBIA

1 Bruce Bawer, "Last Word: Blessings or Earnings?" *The Advocate*, April 28, 1998.

2 Schwartz, "With or Against Us."

3 Herek, Gillis and Cogan, "Internalized Stigma among Sexual Minority Adults."

4 Barton, "'Abomination'," 477.

5 Ganzevoort, van der Laan and Olsman, "Growing Up Gay and Religious."

CHAPTER 13: BULLYING

1 "Judy Shepard Spreads the Love on this issue's SoapBox, Instinct Magazine, November 23, 2009.

2 Tolan, "International Trends in Bullying and Children's Health."

3 Berlan et al., "Sexual Orientation and Bullying among Adolescents."

4 Birkett, Espelage and Koenig, "LGB and Questioning Students in Schools."

5 Birkett, Espelage and Koenig, "LGB and Questioning Students in Schools"; D'Augelli, Grossman and Starks, "Childhood Gender Atypicality."

6 Toomey et al., "Gender-Nonconforming Lesbian, Gay, Bisexual, and Transgender Youth."

7 Grant et al., "Injustice at Every Turn"; Sausa, "Translating Research into Practice."

8 Kosciw, Diaz and Greytak, "The 2007 National School Climate Survey."

9 D'Augelli, Grossman and Starks, "Childhood Gender Atypicality."

10 Birkett, Espelage and Koenig, "LGB and Questioning Students in Schools."

11 Storey et al., "Eyes on Bullying."

12 Gini and Pozzoli, "Association between Bullying and Psychosomatic Problems."

13 Campbell and Morrison, "The Relationship Between Bullying, Psychotic-Like Experiences"; Roberts et al., "Pervasive Trauma Exposure."

14 Sourander et al., "Psychosocial Risk Factors Associated with Cyberbullying."

15 Mitchell et al., "Youth Internet Victimization."

16 Birkett, Espelage and Koenig, "LGB and Questioning Students in Schools."

17 Ttofi and Farrington, "Effectiveness of School-Based Programs to Reduce Bullying."

18 Centers for Disease Control and Prevention, "Lesbian, Gay, Bisexual, and Transgender Health."

19 Arseneault, Bowes and Shakoor, "Bullying Victimization in Youths and Mental Health Problems."

CHAPTER 14: CAN SEXUAL ORIENTATION BE CHANGED?

1 Kinsey, Pomeroy, Martin and Gebhard, *Sexual Behavior in the Human Female*, 447.
2 Reinisch, *The Kinsey Institute New Report on Sex*, 141.
3 Gold et al., "Psychological Outcomes among Lesbian Sexual Assault Survivors."
4 Wilson, Zeng and Blackburn, "An Examination of Parental Attachments."
5 Kendall-Tackett and Becker-Blease, "The Importance of Retrospective Findings."
6 Grimbos et al., "Sexual Orientation and the Second to Fourth Finger Length Ratio"; Bailey and Pillard, "A Genetic Study of Male Sexual Orientation"; Kallman, "Comparative Twin Study on the Genetic Aspects."
7 Jannini et al., "Male Homosexuality"; Mustanski, Chivers and Bailey, "A Critical Review of Recent Biological Research"; Schiavi and White, "Androgens and Male Sexual Function."
8 Haider-Markel and Joslyn, "Beliefs about the Origins of Homosexuality."
9 Drescher, "I'm Your Handyman."
10 APA Task Force on Appropriate Therapeutic Responses to Sexual Orientation, *Report of the Task Force*, 66.
11 Herek and Garnets, "Sexual Orientation and Mental Health."
12 Beckstead, "Can We Change Sexual Orientation?"

PART III: THE PATH TO HEALTHY ADULTHOOD

CHAPTER 15: SOCIAL-EMOTIONAL DEVELOPMENT

1 Erikson, *Identity and the Life Cycle*.

CHAPTER 16: THE ONLY WAY THROUGH IS OUT

1 Valerie Strauss, "The Funniest Commencement Speeches," *Washington Post*, May 9, 2010.
2 LaSala, "Gay Male Couples"; Lewis et al., "An Empirical Analysis of Stressors"; Halpin and Allen, "Changes in Psychosocial Well-Being"; Stevens, "Understanding Gay Identity Development"; Savin-Williams, *Mom, Dad, I'm Gay*.
3 Mohr and Fassinger, "Sexual Orientation Identity and Romantic Relationship Quality."
4 Vaughan and Waehler, "Coming Out Growth."
5 Cole et al., "Elevated Physical Health Risk among Gay Men"; Morris, Waldo and Rothblum, "A Model of Predictors and Outcomes of Outness"; Ragins, Singh and Cornwell, "Making the Invisible Visible."
6 Critcher and Ferguson, "Concealment and Ego Depletion."
7 Legate, Ryan and Weinstein, "Is Coming Out Always a 'Good Thing'?"

8   D'Augelli, "Developmental and Contextual Factors and Mental Health"; D'Augelli and Grossman, "Disclosure of Sexual Orientation, Victimization, and Mental Health."

9   Grov et al., "Race, Ethnicity, Gender, and Generational Factors"; Savin-Williams, *The New Gay Teenager.*

10 Floyd and Bakeman, "Coming-Out Across the Life Course."

11 Weinberg, Williams and Pryor, *Dual Attraction.*

12 Fox, "Bisexual Identities."

13 Bogaert and Hafer, "Predicting the Timing of Coming Out in Gay and Bisexual Men."

14 Doty et al., "Sexuality Related Social Support."

15 D'Augelli and Patterson, *Lesbian, Gay, and Bisexual Identities over the Lifespan*; D'Augelli, Grossman and Starks, "Parents' Awareness of Lesbian, Gay, and Bisexual Youths' Sexual Orientation."

16 Heatherington and Lavner, "Coming to Terms with Coming Out."

17 Potieczniak, Crosbie-Burnett and Saltzburg, "Experiences Regarding Coming Out to Parents."

18 Claudia Dreifus, *Interview*, New York: Seven Stories Press, 1997.

19 Schwartz, "With or Against Us."

20 Meyer, "Identity, Stress, and Resiliency."

21 Haas et al., "Suicide and Suicide Risk."

22 Meyer, "Identity, Stress, and Resiliency."

CHAPTER 17: STAGES OF COMING OUT

1   Cass, "Homosexual Identity Formation."

CHAPTER 18: WHEN DEVELOPMENT DERAILS

1   Heatherington and Lavner, "Coming to Terms with Coming Out."

2   Ibid.

3   Holtzen, Kenny and Mahalik, "Contributions of Parental Attachment."

CHAPTER 19: RESILIENCY AND HOPE

1   Knight, "A Resilience Framework."

2   Borowsky, Ireland and Resnick, "Adolescent Suicide Attempts"; Rostosky et al., "Is Religiosity a Protective Factor"; Goodenow, Szalacha and Westheimer, "School Support Groups."

3   Saewyc et al., "Stigma Management?"

4   Doty et al., "Sexuality Related Social Support."

5   Herrick et al., "Resilience as an Untapped Resource."

6   Lee et al., "Resiliency and Survival Skills among Newly Homeless Adolescents"; Milburn et al., "Cross-National Variations in Behavioral Profiles."

7   Legate, Ryan and Weinstein, "Is Coming Out Always a 'Good Thing'?"
8   Szymanski, Kashubeck-West and Meyer, "Internalized Heterosexism."

PART IV: HEALTH AND SEXUALITY

CHAPTER 20: SEXUALITY: THE BIRDS AND THE BEES REVISITED

1   Chandra et al., "Sexual Behavior, Sexual Attraction, and Sexual Identity."
2   Mathy et al., "Methodological Rigor with Internet Samples."
3   Kinsey, Pomeroy, Martin and Gebhard, *Sexual Behavior in the Human Female*, 448–450.
4   Kinsey, Pomeroy and Martin, *Sexual Behavior in the Human Male*, 639.
5   Reinisch, *The Kinsey Institute New Report on Sex.*
6   Hite, *The Hite Report on Male Sexuality*; Hite, *The Hite Report: A Nationwide Study of Female Sexuality.*
7   Hite, *The Hite Report on Male Sexuality*, 45.
8   Ibid., 811.
9   Ibid.
10 Hite, *The Hite Report: A Nationwide Study of Female Sexuality.*

CHAPTER 21: HEALTH RISKS

1   Pascoe and Richman, "Perceived Discrimination and Health."
2   Meyer, Dietrich and Schwartz, "Lifetime Prevalence of Mental Disorders and Suicide Attempts."
3   Ibid.
4   Bostwick et al., "Dimensions of Sexual Orientation"; Herek and Garnets, "Sexual Orientation and Mental Health"; Meyer, "Minority Stress and Mental Health in Gay Men"; Lee, Griffin and Melvin, "Tobacco Use among Sexual Minorities"; Struble et al., "Overweight and Obesity"; Wilson, Zeng and Blackburn, "An Examination of Parental Attachments"; Haas et al., "Suicide and Suicide Risk"; Hall et al., "Estimation of HIV Incidence"; El-Sadr, Mayer and Hodder, "AIDS in America."
5   Marshal et al., "Sexual Orientation and Adolescent Substance Use."
6   McCabe et al., "Sexual Orientation, Substance Use Behaviors."
7   Lee, Griffin and Melvin, "Tobacco Use among Sexual Minorities."
8   Struble et al., "Overweight and Obesity."
9   Barnett, "Trends in Obesity Prevalence and Associated Health Risk Behaviors."
10 Austin et al., "Sexual Orientation Disparities in Weight Status in Adolescence"; Deputy and Boehmer, "Determinants of Body Weight."
11 Saewyc et al., "Sexual Intercourse, Abuse and Pregnancy."
12 Haas et al., "Suicide and Suicide Risk."
13 Remafedi, Farrow and Deisher, "Risk Factors for Attempted Suicide."
14 Haas et al., "Suicide and Suicide Risk."

15 King et al., "A Systematic Review of Mental Disorder."
16 Russell and Joyner, "Adolescent Sexual Orientation and Suicide Risk."
17 Kruks, "Gay and Lesbian Homeless/Street Youth."
18 Haas et al., "Suicide and Suicide Risk."
19 Grant et al., "Injustice at Every Turn."
20 Herbst et al., "Estimating HIV Prevalence and Risk Behaviors."
21 Padilla, Crisp and Rew, "Parental Acceptance and Illegal Drug Use."
22 Ryan et al., "Family Rejections as a Predictor of Negative Health Outcomes."
23 Kubler-Ross, *On Death and Dying.*

CHAPTER 22: OPTIMIZING HEALTH CARE

1 Obedin-Maliver et al., "Lesbian, Gay, Bisexual, and Transgender-Related Content."
2 Kreiss and Patterson, "Psychosocial Issues in Primary Care"; Kitts, "Barriers to Optimal Care."
3 Dohrenwend and Sharp, "Lesbian and Bisexual Health Survey."
4 Katherine A. O'Hanlan, "Top 10 Things Lesbians Should Discuss with Their Health Care Provider," San Francisco: Gay and Lesbian Medical Association; Vincent MB Silenzio, "Top 10 Things Gay Men Should Discuss with Their Health Care Provider," San Francisco: Gay and Lesbian Medical Association; Rebecca A. Allison, "Top 10 Things Transgender Persons Should Discuss with Their Health Care Provider," San Francisco: Gay and Lesbian Medical Association.
5 Kim, "Weighing the Benefits and Costs of HPV Vaccination."

CHAPTER 23: BECOMING AN IN-LAW AND GRANDPARENT

1 Fitzgerald, "Children of Lesbian and Gay Parents."

PART V: THE FIGHT FOR EQUALITY

CHAPTER 25: MARRIAGE MATTERS

1 O'Connell and Feliz, "Same-Sex Couple Household Statistics."
2 Renna, "Williams Institute Experts Comment."
3 Lofquist, "Same-Sex Couple Households."
4 Pew Forum on Religion and Public Life, "Religion and Attitudes Toward Same-Sex Marriage."
5 Wood, Goesling and Avellar, *The Effects of Marriage on Health.*
6 Riggle and Rostosky, "The Consequences of Marriage Policy."
7 Rostosky et al., "Marriage Amendments and Psychological Distress."

CHAPTER 27: POSITIVELY GAY

1 Sullivan, "Why Gay Marriage Is Good for Straight America."
2 Bybee et al., "Are Gay Men in Worse Mental Health Than Heterosexual Men?"
3 D'Augelli and Grossman, "Disclosure of Sexual Orientation."
4 Riggle et al., "The Positive Aspects of Being a Lesbian or Gay Man."

BIBLIOGRAPHY

Adams, Henry E., Lester W. Wright, Jr. and Bethany A. Lohr. "Is Homophobia Associated with Homosexual Arousal?" *Journal of Abnormal Psychology* 105 (1996): 440–445.

American Psychological Association. "Guidelines for Psychological Practice with Lesbian, Gay, and Bisexual Clients." *American Psychologist* 67 (2012): 10–42.

APA Task Force on Appropriate Therapeutic Responses to Sexual Orientation. *Report of the Task Force on Appropriate Therapeutic Responses to Sexual Orientation.* Washington, DC: American Psychological Association, 2009. www.apa.org/pi/lgbt/resources/therapeutic-response.pdf.

Arm, Jennifer R., Sharon Horne and Heidi M. Levitt. "Negotiating Connection to GLBT Experience: Family Members' Experience of Anti-GLBT Movements and Policies." *Journal of Counseling Psychology* 56 (2009): 82–96.

Arseneault, Louise, Lucy Bowes and Sania Shakoor. "Bullying Victimization in Youths and Mental Health Problems: 'Much Ado About Nothing'?" *Psychological Medicine* 40 (2010): 717–729.

Ashmore, Richard D. and Frances K. Del Boca. "Conceptual Approaches to Stereotypes and Stereotyping." In *Cognitive Processes in Stereotyping an Intergroup Behavior* edited by David L. Hamilton. Hillsdale, NJ: Lawrence Erlbaum Associates, 1981.

Atkinson, P.A., C.R. Martin and J. Rankin. "Resilience Revisited." *Journal of Psychiatric and Mental Health Nursing* 16 (2009): 137–145.

Austin, S. Bryn, Najat J. Ziyadeh, Heather L. Corliss, Jess Haines, Helaine Rockett, David Wypij and Alison E. Field. "Sexual Orientation Disparities in Weight Status in Adolescence: Findings from a Prospective Study." *Obesity* 17 (2009): 1776–1782.

Bailey, J. Michael and Richard C. Pillard. "A Genetic Study of Male Sexual Orientation." *Archives of General Psychiatry* 48 (1991): 1089–1096.

Barnett, Corrie. "Trends in Obesity Prevalence and Associated Health Risk Behaviors among College Women in the United States." Dissertation, University of South Carolina, 2009. ProQuest (AAT3352729).

Barton, Bernadette. "'Abomination': Life as a Bible Belt Gay." *Journal of Homosexuality* 57 (2010): 465–484.

Beckstead, A. Lee. "Can We Change Sexual Orientation?" *Archives of Sexual Behavior* 41 (2012): 121–134.

Beeler, Jeff and Vicky DiProva. "Family Adjustment Following Disclosure of Homosexuality by a Member: Themes Discerned in Narrative Accounts." *Journal of Marital and Family Therapy* 25 (1999): 443–459.

Bekaert, Sarah. "Tackling Homophobic Attitudes and Bullying in Youth Settings." *Paediatric Nursing* 22 (2010): 27–9.

Bell, Alan P., Martin S. Weinberg and Sue Kiefer Hammersmith. *Sexual Preference: Its Development in Men and Women.* Bloomington, Indiana: Indiana University Press, 1981.

Berlan, Elise D., Heather L. Corliss, Alison E. Field, Elizabeth Goodman and S. Bryn Austin. "Sexual Orientation and Bullying among Adolescents in the Growing Up Today Study." *Journal of Adolescent Health* 46 (2010): 366–371.

Birkett, Michelle, Dorothy L. Espelage and Brian Koenig. "LGB and Questioning Students in Schools: The Moderating Effects of Homophobic Bullying and School Climate on Negative Outcomes." *Journal of Youth Adolescence* 38 (2009): 989–1000.

Blake, Susan M., Rebecca Ledsky, Thomas Lehman, Carol Goodenow, Richard Sawyer and Tim Hack. "Preventing Sexual Risk Behaviors among Gay, Lesbian, and Bisexual Adolescents: The Benefits of Gay-Sensitive HIV Instruction in Schools." *American Journal of Public Health* 91 (2001): 940–946.

Boehmer, Ulrike. "Twenty Years of Public Health Research: Inclusion of Lesbian, Gay, Bisexual, and Transgender Populations." *American Journal of Public Health* 92 (2002): 1125–1130.

Bogaert, Anthony F. and Carolyn Hafer. "Predicting the Timing of Coming Out in Gay and Bisexual Men from World Beliefs, Physical Attractiveness, and Childhood Gender Identity/Role." *Journal of Applied Social Psychology* 39 (2009): 1991–2019.

Bontempo, Daniel E. and Anthony R. D'Augelli. "Effects of At-School Victimization and Sexual Orientation on Lesbian, Gay, or Bisexual Youths' Health Risk Behavior." *Journal of Adolescence Health* 30 (2002): 363–374.

Borowsky, Iris Wagman, Marjorie Ireland and Michael D. Resnick. "Adolescent Suicide Attempts: Risks and Protectors." *Pediatrics* 107 (2001): 485–493.

Bostwick, Wendy B., Carol J. Boyd, Tonda L. Hughes and Sean Esteban McCabe. "Dimensions of Sexual Orientation and the Prevalence of Mood and Anxiety Disorders in the United States." *American Journal of Public Health* 100 (2010): 468–475.

Bouris, Alida, Vincent Guilamo-Ramos, Angela Pickard, Chengshi Shiu, Penny S. Loosier, Patricia Dittus, Kari Gloppen and J. Michael Waldmiller. "A Systematic Review of Parental Influences on the Health and Well-Being of Lesbian, Gay, and Bisexual Youth: Time for a New Public Health Research and Practice Agenda." *Journal of Primary Prevention* 31 (2010): 273–309.

Bowes, Lucy, Barbara Maughan, Avshalom Caspi, Terrie E. Moffitt and Louise Arseneault. "Families Promote Emotional and Behavioral Resilience to Bullying: Evidence of an Environmental Effect." *Journal of Child Psychology and Psychiatry* 51 (2010): 809–817.

Brown, Michael J. and Jennifer L. Groscup. "Homophobia and Acceptance of Stereotypes about Gays and Lesbians." *Individual Differences Research* 7 (2009): 159–167.

Buchmueller, Thomas and Christopher S. Carpenter. "Disparities in Health Insurance Coverage, Access, and Outcomes for Individuals in Same-Sex Versus Different-Sex Relationships, 2000–2007." *American Journal of Public Health* 100 (2010): 489–95.

Bybee, Jane A., Eric L. Sullivan, Erich Zielonka and Elizabeth Moes. "Are Gay Men in Worse Mental Health Than Heterosexual Men? The Role of Age, Shame and Guilt, and Coming Out." *Journal of Adult Development* 16 (2009): 144–154.

Campbell, Michelle L.C. and Anthony P. Morrison. "The Relationship Between Bullying, Psychotic-Like Experiences and Appraisals in 14–16-Year Olds." *Behavior Research and Therapy* 45 (2007): 1579–1591.

Cass, Vivienne. "Homosexual Identity Formation: A Theoretical Model." *Journal of Homosexuality* 4 (1979): 219–235.

Centers for Disease Control and Prevention. "Lesbian, Gay, Bisexual, and Transgender Health." May 2011. www.cdc.gov/lgbthealth/youth.htm.

Chandra, Anjani, William D. Mosher, Casey Copen and Catlainn Sionean. "Sexual Behavior, Sexual Attraction, and Sexual Identity in the United States: Data from the 2006–2008 National Survey of Family Growth." *National Health Statistics Report* 36 (2011): 1–16. www.cdc. gov/nchs/data/nhsr/nhsr036. pdf.

Clements-Nolle, Kristen, Rani Marx and Mitchell Katz. "Attempted Suicide among Transgender Persons: The Influence of Gender-Based Discrimination and Victimization." *Journal of Homosexuality* 51 (2006): 53–69.

Coker, Tumaini R., S. Bryn Austin and Mark A. Schuster. "The Health and Health Care of Lesbian, Gay, and Bisexual Adolescents." *Annual Review of Public Health* 31 (2010): 457–477.

Cole, Steve W., Margaret E. Kemeny, Shelley E. Taylor and Barbara R. Visscher. "Elevated Physical Health Risk among Gay Men Who Conceal Their Homosexual Identity." *Health Psychology* 15 (1996): 243–251.

Cramer, Robert J., Frank D. Golom, Charles T. LoPresto and Shalene M. Kirkley. "Weighing the Evidence: Empirical Assessment and Ethical Implications of Conversion Therapy." *Ethics and Behavior* 18 (2008): 93–114.

Critcher, Clayton R. and Melissa J. Ferguson. "Concealment and Ego Depletion: Does 'Don't Ask, Don't Tell' Hinder Performance?" Paper presented at the meeting for the Society for Personality and Social Psychology, San Antonio, TX, 2011.

D'Augelli, Anthony R. "Developmental and Contextual Factors and Mental Health among Lesbian, Gay, and Bisexual Youths." In *Sexual Orientation and Mental Health: Examining Identity and Development in Lesbian, Gay, and Bisexual People*, edited by Allen Martin Omoto and Howard S. Kurtzman, 37–53. Washington, DC: APA Books, 2006.

D'Augelli, Anthony R. and Arnold H. Grossman. "Disclosure of Sexual Orientation, Victimization, and Mental Health among Lesbian, Gay, and Bisexual Older Adults." *Journal of Interpersonal Violence* 16 (2001): 1008–1027.

D'Augelli, Anthony R. and Charlotte J. Patterson, eds. *Lesbian, Gay, and Bisexual Identities over the Lifespan: Psychological Perspectives*. New York: Oxford University Press, 1995.

D'Augelli, Anthony R., Arnold H. Grossman and Michael T. Starks. "Childhood Gender Atypicality, Victimization, and PTSD among Lesbian, Gay, and Bisexual Youth." *Journal of Interpersonal Violence* 21 (2006): 1462–1482.

———. "Parents' Awareness of Lesbian, Gay, and Bisexual Youths' Sexual Orientation." *Journal of Marriage and Family* 67 (2005): 474–482.

D'Augelli, Anthony R., Arnold H. Grossman, Scott L. Hershberger and Timothy S. O'Connell. "Aspects of Mental Health among Older Lesbian, Gay, and Bisexual Adults." *Aging & Mental Health* 5 (2001): 149–158.

Deputy, Nicholas P. and Ulrike Boehmer. "Determinants of Body Weight among Men of Different Sexual Orientation." *Preventive Medicine* 52 (2010): 129–131.

Dohrenwend, Anne and L. Sharp. "Lesbian and Bisexual Health Survey." Paper presented at the National Lesbian Health Conference, San Francisco, CA, June 23, 2001.

Doty, Nathan Daniel, Brian L.B. Willoughby, Kristin M. Lindahl and Neena M. Malik. "Sexuality Related Social Support among Lesbian, Gay, and Bisexual Youth." *Journal of Youth and Adolescence* 39 (2010): 1134–1147.

Drescher, Jack. "I'm Your Handyman: A History of Reparative Therapies." *Journal of Homosexuality* 36 (1998): 19–42.

Eisenberg, Marla E. and Michael D. Resnick. "Suicidality among Gay, Lesbian and Bisexual Youth: The Role of Protective Factors." *Journal of Adolescent Health* 39 (2006): 662–668.

El-Sadr, Wafaa M., Kenneth H. Mayer and Sally L. Hodder. "AIDS in America: Forgotten But Not Gone." *New England Journal of Medicine* 362 (2010): 967–70.

Erikson, Erik H. *Identity and the Life Cycle*. New York: International Universities Press, 1959.

Espelage, Dorothy L., Steven R. Aragon and Michelle Birkett. "Homophobic Teasing, Psychological Outcomes, and Sexual Orientation among High School Students: What Influence Do Parents and Schools Have?" *School Psychology Review* 37 (2008): 202–216. 8.

Fagan, Peter J., Thomas N. Wise, Chester W. Schmidt and Fred S. Berlin, "Pedophilia," *Journal of the American Medical Association* 288 (2002): 2458–2465.

Federal Bureau of Investigation. "Uniform Crime Report: About Hate Crime Statistics, 2010." US Department of Justice. www.fbi.gov/about-us/cjis/ucr/hate-crime/2010.

Fergusson, David M., L. John Horwood and Annette L. Beautrais. "Is Sexual Orientation Related to Mental Health Problems and Suicidality in Young People?" *Archives of General Psychiatry* 56 (1999): 876–880.

Fergusson, David M., L. John Horwood, Elizabeth M. Ridder and Annette L. Beautrais. "Sexual Orientation and Mental Health in a Birth Cohort of Young Adults." *Psychological Medicine* 35 (2005): 971–981.

Finkelhor, David, Richard Ormrod, Heather Turner and Sherry L. Hamby. "The Victimization of Children and Youth: A Comprehensive National Survey." *Child Maltreatment* 10 (2005): 5–25.

Finlay, Barbara and Carol S. Walther. "The Relation of Religious Affiliation, Service Attendance, and Other Factors to Homophobic Attitudes among University Students." *Review of Religious Research* 44 (2003): 370–393.

Fitzgerald, Bridget. "Children of Lesbian and Gay Parents: A Review of the Literature." *Marriage and Family Review* 29 (1999): 57–75.

Floyd, Frank J. and Roger Bakeman. "Coming-Out Across the Life Course: Implications and Historical Context." *Archives of Sexual Behavior* 35 (2006): 287–296.

Fox, Ronald C. "Bisexual Identities." In *Lesbian, Gay, and Bisexual Identities over the Lifespan; Psychological Perspectives*, edited by Anthony R. D'Augelli and Charlotte J. Patterson, 48–86. New York: Oxford University Press, 1995.

Frost, David M. and Ilan H. Meyer. "Internalized Homophobia and Relationship Quality among Lesbians, Gay Men, and Bisexuals." *Journal of Counseling Psychology* 56 (2009): 97–109.

Ganzevoort, R. Ruard, Mark van der Laan and Erik Olsman. "Growing Up Gay and Religious. Conflict, Dialogue, and Religious Identity Strategies." *Mental Health, Religion and Culture* 14 (2011): 209–222.

Gattis, Maurice N. "Psychosocial Problems Associated with Homelessness in Sexual Minority Youths." *Journal of Human Behavior in the Social Environment* 19 (2009): 1066–1094.

Gay and Lesbian Medical Association and LGBT Health Experts. *Healthy People 2010 Companion Document for Lesbian, Gay, Bisexual, and Transgender (LGBT) Health*. San Francisco, CA: Gay and Lesbian Medical Association, 2001. www.glma.org/_data/n_0001/resources/live/HealthyCompanionDoc3.pdf.

Gilman, Stephen E., Susan D. Cochran, Vickie M. Mays, Michael Hughes, David Ostrow and Ronald C. Kessler. "Risk of Psychiatric Disorders among Individuals Reporting Same-Sex Sexual Partners in a National Comorbidity Survey." *American Journal of Public Health* 91 (2001): 933–939.

Gini, Gianluca and Tiziana Pozzoli. "Association between Bullying and Psychosomatic Problems: A Meta-Analysis." *Pediatrics* 123 (2009): 1059–1065.

Ginicola, Misty M. and Cheri Smith. "The Church, the Closet, and the Couch: The Counselor's Role in Assisting Clients to Integrate Their Sexual Orientation and Religious Identity." *Journal of LGBT Issues in Counseling* 5 (2011): 304–326.

Gold, Sari D., Benjamin D. Dickstein, Brian P. Marx and Jennifer M. Lexington "Psychological Outcomes among Lesbian Sexual Assault Survivors: An Examination of the Roles of Internalized Homophobia and Experiential Avoidance." *Psychology of Women Quarterly* 33 (2009). 54–66.

Gold, Shaunna Payne and Dafina Lazarus Stewart. "Lesbian, Gay, and Bisexual Students Coming Out at the Intersection of Spirituality and Sexual Identity." *Journal of LGBT Issues in Counseling* 5 (2011): 237–258.

Goldberg, Abbie E. and Katherine A. Kuvalanka. "Marriage (In)equality: The Perspectives of Adolescents and Emerging Adults with Lesbian, Gay, and Bisexual Parents." *Journal of Marriage and Family* 74 (2012): 34–52.

Goodenow, Carol, Laura Szalacha and Kim Westheimer. "School Support Groups, Other School Factors, and the Safety of Sexual Minority Adolescents." *Psychology in the Schools* 43 (2006): 573–89.

Grant, Jaime M., Lisa A. Mottet, Justin Tanis, Jack Harrison, Jody L. Herman and Mara Keisling. "Injustice at Every Turn: A Report of the National Transgender Discrimination Survey, Executive Summary." Washington: National Center for Transgender Equality and National Gay and Lesbian Task Force, 2011.

Grimbos, Teresa, Khytam Dawood, Robert P. Burriss, Kenneth J. Zucker and David A. Puts. "Sexual Orientation and the Second to Fourth Finger Length Ratio: A Meta-Analysis in Men and Women." *Behavioral Neuroscience* 124 (2010): 278–287.

Grossman, Arnold H. and Anthony R. D'Augelli. "Transgender Youth: Invisible and Vulnerable." *Journal of Homosexuality* 51 (2006): 111–128.

Grov, Christian, David S. Bimbi, Jose E. Nanin and Jeffrey T. Parsons. "Race, Ethnicity, Gender, and Generational Factors Associated with the Coming-Out Process among Lesbian, and Bisexual Individuals." *Journal of Sex Research* 43 (2006): 115–121.

Haas, Ann P., Mickey Eliason, Vickie M. Mays, Robin M. Mathy, Susan D. Cochran, Anthony R. D'Augelli, Morton M. Silverman, Prudence W. Fisher, Tonda Hughes, Margaret Rosario, Stephen T. Russell, Effie Malley, Jerry Reed, David A. Litts, Ellen Haller, Randall L. Sell, Gary Remafedi, Judith Bradford, Annette L. Beautrais, Gregory K. Brown, Gary M. Diamond, Mark S. Friedman, Robert Garofalo, Mason S. Turner, Amber Hollibaugh and Paula J. Clayton. "Suicide and Suicide Risk in Lesbian, Gay, Bisexual, and Transgender Populations: Review and Recommendations." *Journal of Homosexuality* 58 (2011): 10–51.

Haider-Markel, Donald P. and Mark R. Joslyn. "Beliefs about the Origins of Homosexuality and Support for Gay Rights: An Empirical Test of Attribution Theory." *Public Opinion Quarterly* 72 (2008): 291–310.

Hall, H. Irene, Ruiguang Song, Philip Rhodes, Joseph Prejean, Qian An, Lisa M. Lee, John Karon, Ron Brookmeyer, Edward H. Kaplan, Matthew T. McKenna and Robert S. Janssen. "Estimation of HIV Incidence in the United States." *Journal of the American Medical Association* 300 (2008): 520–9.

Hall, Ryan C.W. and Richard C.W. Hall. "A Profile of Pedophilia: Definition, Characteristics of Offenders, Recidivism, Treatment Outcomes, and Forensic Issues." *Mayo Clinic Proceedings* 82 (2007): 457–471.

Halpin, Sean A. and Michael W. Allen. "Changes in Psychosocial Well-Being During Stages of Gay Identity Development." *Journal of Homosexuality* 47 (2004): 109–126.

Hansen, Jennifer E. and Serena M. Lambert. "Grief and Loss of Religion: The Experiences of Four Rural Lesbians." *Journal of Lesbian Studies* 15 (2011): 187–196.

Healthy People 2020. "Lesbian, Gay, Bisexual, and Transgender Health." Washington, DC: US Department of Health and Human Services, 2012. www.healthypeople.gov/2020/topicsobjectives2020/overview.aspx?topic id=25#.

Heatherington, Laurie and Justin A. Lavner. "Coming to Terms with Coming Out: Review and Recommendations for Family Systems-Focused Research." *Journal of Family Psychology* 22 (2008): 329–343.

Herbst, Jeffrey H., Elizabeth D. Jacobs, Teresa J. Finlayson, Vel S. McKleroy, Mary Spink Neumann and Nicole Crepaz. "Estimating HIV Prevalence and Risk Behaviors of Transgender Persons in the United States: A Systematic Review." *AIDS and Behavior* 12 (2008): 1–17.

Herek, Gregory M. "Legal Recognition of Same-Sex Relationships in the United States: A Social Science Perspective." *American Psychologist* 61 (2006): 607–621.

Herek, Gregory M. and John P. Capitanio. "'Some of My Best Friends': Intergroup Contact, Concealable Stigma, and Heterosexuals' Attitudes Toward Gay Men and Lesbians." *Personality and Social Psychology Bulletin* 22 (1996): 412–424.

Herek, Gregory M. and Linda D. Garnets. "Sexual Orientation and Mental Health." *Annual Review of Clinical Psychology* 3 (2007): 353–75.

Herek, Gregory M., J. Roy Gillis and Jeanine C. Cogan. "Psychological Sequelae of Hate Crime Victimization among Lesbian, Gay, and Bisexual Adults." *Journal of Consulting Clinical Psychology* 67 (1999): 945–951.

———. "Internalized Stigma among Sexual Minority Adults: Insights from a Social Psychological Perspective." *Journal of Counseling Psychology* 56 (2009): 32–43.

Herrick, Amy L., Sin How Lim, Chongyi Wei, Helen Smith, Thomas Guadamuz, Mark S. Friedman and Ron Stall. "Resilience as an Untapped Resource in Behavioral Intervention Design for Gay Men." *AIDS and Behavior* 15 (2011): S25-S29.

Hite, Shere. *The Hite Report: A Nationwide Study of Female Sexuality*. New York: Macmillan, 1976.

———. *The Hite Report on Male Sexuality*. New York: Alfred A. Knopf, 1981.

Holtzen, David W., Maureen E. Kenny and James R. Mahalik. "Contributions of Parental Attachment to Gay or Lesbian Disclosure to Parents and Dysfunctional Cognitive Processes." *Journal of Counseling Psychology* 42 (1995): 350–355.

Hughes, Tonda L. "Lesbians' Drinking Patterns: Beyond the Data." *Substance Use and Misuse* 38 (2003): 1739–1758.

Human Rights Campaign. "Answers to Questions about Marriage Equality." Washington, DC: Human Rights Campaign, 2004.

Ibanez, Gladys E., David W. Purcell, Ron Stall, Jeffrey T. Parsons and Cynthia A. Gómez. "Sexual Risk, Substance Use, and Psychological Distress in HIV-Positive Gay and Bisexual Men Who Also Inject Drugs." *AIDS* 19 (2005): 49–55.

Jannini, Emmanuele A., Ray Blanchard, Andrea Camperio-Ciani and John Bancroft. "Male Homosexuality: Nature or Culture?" *Journal of Sexual Medicine* 7 (2010): 3245–3253.

Kahn, Kimberly B. and Adam W. Fingerhut. "Essentialist Beliefs and Sexual Prejudice against Gay Men: Divergence at the Levels of Categories versus Traits." *Psychology and Sexuality* 2 (2011): 137–146.

Kallman, Franz J. "Comparative Twin Study on the Genetic Aspects of Male Homosexuality." *Journal of Nervous and Mental Disease.* 115 (1952): 283–298.

Kendall-Tackett, Kathleen and Kathryn Becker-Blease. "The Importance of Retrospective Findings in Child Maltreatment Research." *Child Abuse and Neglect* 28 (2004): 723–727.

Kim, Jane J. "Weighing the Benefits and Costs of HPV Vaccination of Young Men." *New England Journal of Medicine* 364 (2011): 393–395.

King, Michael, Joanna Semlyen, Sharon See Tai, Helen Killaspy, David Osborn, Dmitri Popelyuk and Irwin Nazareth. "A Systematic Review of Mental Disorder, Suicide, and Deliberate Self Harm in Lesbian, Gay, and Bisexual People." *BMC Psychiatry* 8 (2008): 70.

Kinsey, Alfred C., Wardell B. Pomeroy and Clyde E. Martin. *Sexual Behavior in the Human Male.* Philadelphia, PA: W. B. Saunders, 1948.

Kinsey, Alfred C., Wardell B. Pomeroy, Clyde E. Martin and Paul H. Gebhard. *Sexual Behavior in the Human Female.* Philadelphia, PA: W. B. Saunders; 1953.

Kitts, Robert L. "Barriers to Optimal Care between Physicians and Lesbians, Gay, Bisexual, Transgender, and Questioning Patients." *Journal of Homosexuality* 57 (2010): 730–747.

Knight, Cecily. "A Resilience Framework: Perspectives for Educators." *Health Education* 107 (2007): 543–555.

Kosciw, Joseph G., Elizabeth M. Diaz and Emily A. Greytak. "The 2007 National School Climate Survey: The Experiences of Lesbian, Gay, Bisexual, and Transgender Youth in Our Nation's Schools." New York, NY: Gay, Lesbian and Straight Education Network, 2008. www.glsen.org/binary-data/GLSEN_ATTACHMENTS/file/000/001/1290-1.pdf.

Kreiss, J.L. and D.L. Patterson. "Psychosocial Issues in Primary Care of Lesbian, Gay, Bisexual, and Transgender Youth." *Journal of Pediatric Health Care* 11 (1997): 266–274.

Krug, Etienne G., Linda L. Dahlberg, James A. Mercy, Anthony B. Zwi and Rafael Lozano, eds. *World Report on Violence and Health*. Geneva: World Health Organization, 2002: 1–44.

Kruks, Gabe. "Gay and Lesbian Homeless/Street Youth: Special Issues and Concerns." *Journal of Adolescent Health* 12 (2010): 515–8.

Kubler-Ross, Elisabeth. *On Death and Dying*. New York: Macmillan, 1969.

LaSala, Michael C. "Gay Male Couples: The Importance of Coming Out and Being Out to Parents." *Journal of Homosexuality* 39 (2000): 47–71.

Lee, Joseph G.L., Gabriel K. Griffin and Cathy L. Melvin. "Tobacco Use among Sexual Minorities, USA, 1987–2007 (May): A systematic review." *Tobacco Control* 18 (2009): 275–82.

Lee, Sung-Jae, Li-Jung Liang, Mary Jane Rotheram-Borus and Norweeta G. Milburn. "Resiliency and Survival Skills among Newly Homeless Adolescents: Implications for Future Interventions." *Vulnerable Children and Youth Studies* 6 (2011): 301–308.

Legate, Nicole, Richard M. Ryan and Netta Weinstein. "Is Coming Out Always a 'Good Thing'? Exploring the Relations of Autonomy Support, Outness, and Wellness for Lesbian, Gay, and Bisexual Individuals." *Social Psychological and Personality Science* (June 2011).

Levitt, Heidi M., Elin Ovrebo, Mollie B. Anderson-Cleveland, Christina Leone, Jae Y. Jeong, Jennifer R. Arm, Beth P. Bonin, John Cicala, Rachel Coleman, Anna Laurie, James M. Vardaman and Sharon G. Horne. "Balancing Dangers: GLBT Experience in a Time of Anti-GLBT Legislation." *Journal of Counseling Psychology* 56 (2009): 67–81.

Levy, Denise L. and Patricia Reeves. "Resolving Identity Conflict: Gay, Lesbian, and Queer Individuals with a Christian Upbringing." *Journal of Gay & Lesbian Social Services* 23 (2011): 53–68.

Lewis, Robin J., Valerian J. Derlega, Andrea Berndt, Lynn M. Morris and Suzana Rose. "An Empirical Analysis of Stressors for Gay Men and Lesbians." *Journal of Homosexuality* 42 (2001): 63–88.

Lofquist, Daphne. "Same-Sex Couple Households." Washington, DC: United States Census Bureau, 2011. www.census.gov/prod/2011pubs/acsbr10–03.pdf.

Maccio, Elaine M. "Self-Reported Sexual Orientation and Identity Before and After Sexual Reorientation Therapy." *Journal of Gay and Lesbian Mental Health* 15 (2011): 242–259.

Makadon, Harvey J. "Ending LGBT Invisibility in Health Care: The First Step in Ensuring Equitable Care." *Cleveland Clinic Journal of Medicine* 78 (2011): 220–223.

Marshal, Michael P., Mark S. Friedman, Ron Stall, Kevin M. King, Jonathan Miles, Melanie A. Gold, Oscar G. Bukstein and Jennifer Q. Morse. "Sexual Orientation and Adolescent Substance Use: A Meta-Analysis and Methodological Review." *Addiction* 103 (2008): 546–556.

Masters, William H., Virginia E. Johnson and Robert C. Kolodny. *Masters and Johnson on Sex and Human Loving*. 2nd ed. Boston, Massachusetts: Little, Brown and Company, 1985: 348–353.

Mathy, Robin M., Marc Schillace, Sarah M. Coleman and Barrie E. Berquist. "Methodological Rigor with Internet Samples: New Ways to Reach Underrepresented Populations." *Cyberpsychology and Behavior* 5 (2002): 253–266.

Mays, Vickie and Susan Cochran. "Mental Health Correlates of Perceived Discrimination among Lesbian, Gay and Bisexual Adults in the United States." *American Journal of Public Health* 91 (2001): 1869–1876.

McCabe, Sean Esteban, Tonda L. Hughes, Wendy B. Bostwick, Brady T. West and Carol J. Boyd. "Sexual Orientation, Substance Use Behaviors and Substance Dependence in the United States." *Addiction* 104 (2009): 1333–1345.

McLaughlin, Katie A., Mark L. Hatzenbuehler and Katherine M. Keyes. "Responses to Discrimination and Psychiatric Disorders among Black, Hispanic, Female, and Lesbian, Gay, and Bisexual Individuals." *American Journal of Public Health* 100 (2010): 1477–84.

Meyer, Ilan H. "Identity, Stress, and Resiliency in Lesbians, Gay Men, and Bisexuals of Color." *The Counseling Psychologist* 38 (2010): 442–454.

———. "Minority Stress and Mental Health in Gay Men." *Journal of Health and Social Behavior* 7 (1995): 9–25.

———. "Prejudice and Discrimination as Social Stressors." In *The Health of Sexual Minorities*, edited by Ilan H. Meyer and Mary E. Northridge. New York, NY: Springer, 2007.

Meyer, Ilan H., Jessica Dietrich and Sharon Schwartz. "Lifetime Prevalence of Mental Disorders and Suicide Attempts in Diverse Lesbian, Gay, and Bisexual Populations." *Research and Practice* 97 (2007): 9–11.

Milburn, Norweeta G., Mary Jane Rotheram-Borus, Eric Rice, Shelley Mallet and Doreen Rosenthal. "Cross-National Variations in Behavioral Profiles among Homeless Youth." *American Journal of Community Psychology* 37 (2006): 63–76.

Mitchell, Kimberly J., David Finkelhor, Janis Wolak, Michele L. Ybarra and Heather Turner. "Youth Internet Victimization in a Broader Victimization Context." *Journal of Adolescent Health* 48 (2011): 128–134.

Mohr, Jonathan J. and Ruth E. Fassinger. "Sexual Orientation Identity and Romantic Relationship Quality in Same-Sex Couples." *Personality and Social Psychology Bulletin* 32 (2006): 1085–1099.

Mohr, Jonathan J. and Matthew S. Kendra. "Revision and Extension of a Multidimensional Measure of Sexual Minority Identity: The Lesbian, Gay, and Bisexual Identity Scale." *Journal of Counseling Psychology* 58 (2011): 234–245.

Morris, Jessica F., Craig R. Waldo and Esther D. Rothblum. "A Model of Predictors and Outcomes of Outness among Lesbian and Bisexual Women." *American Journal of Orthopsychiatry* 71 (2001): 61–71.

Muller, Ann. *Parents Matter: Parents' Relationships with Lesbian Daughters and Gay Sons.* Chicago, IL: Naiad Press, 1987.

Mustanski, Brian S., Meredith L. Chivers and J. Michael Bailey. "A Critical Review of Recent Biological Research on Human Sexual Orientation." *Annual Review of Sex Research* 13 (2002): 89–140.

The National Center for Transgender Equality and the National Gay and Lesbian Task Force. "National Transgender Discrimination Survey." Washington, DC: National Gay and Lesbian Taskforce, 2009. www.thetaskforce.org/downloads/reports/fact_sheets/transsurvey_prelim_findings.pdf.

Newcomb, Michael E. and Brian Mustanski. "Internalized Homophobia and Internalizing Mental Health Problems: A Meta-Analytic Review." *Clinical Psychology Review* 30 (2010): 1019–1029.

Newman, Bernie Sue. "Lesbians, Gays, and Religion: Strategies for Challenging Belief Systems." *Journal of Lesbian Studies* 6 (2002): 87–98.

Newman, Bernie Sue and Peter Gerard Muzzonigro. "The Effects of Traditional Family Values on the Coming Out Process of Gay Male Adolescents." *Adolescence* 28 (1993): 213–26.

Obedin-Maliver, Juno, Elizabeth S. Goldsmith, Leslie Stewart, William White, Eric Tran, Stephanie Brenman, Maggie Wells, David M. Fetterman, Gabriel Garcia and Mitchell R. Lunn. "Lesbian, Gay, Bisexual, and Transgender-Related Content in Undergraduate Medical Education." *Journal of the American Medical Association* 306 (2011): 971–977.

O'Connell, Martin and Sarah Feliz. "Same-Sex Couple Household Statistics from the 2010 Census." Washington, DC: US Bureau of the Census: Social, Economic and Housing Statistics Division, 2011. www.census.gov/hhes/samesex/files/ss-report.doc.

Padilla, Yolanda C., Catherine Crisp and Donna Lynn Rew. "Parental Acceptance and Illegal Drug Use among Gay, Lesbian, and Bisexual Adolescents: Results from a National Survey." *Social Work* 55 (2010): 265–275.

Pascoe, Elizabeth A. and Laura Smart Richman. "Perceived Discrimination and Health: A Meta-Analytic Review." *Psychological Bulletin* 135 (2009): 531–54.

Paul, Jay P., Joseph Catania, Lance Pollack, Judith Moskowitz, Jesse Canchola, Thomas Mills, Diane Binson and Ron Stall. "Suicide Attempts among Gay and Bisexual Men: Lifetime Prevalence and Antecedents." *American Journal of Public Health* 92 (2002): 1338–1345.

Pew Forum on Religion and Public Life. "Religion and Attitudes Toward Same-Sex Marriage." Pew Research Center, February 2012. www.pewforum.org/Gay-Marriage-and-Homosexuality/Religion-and-Attitudes-Toward-Same-Sex-Marriage.aspx.

Potoczniak, Daniel, Margaret Crosbie-Burnett and Nikki Saltzburg. "Experiences Regarding Coming Out to Parents among African American, Hispanic, and White Gay, Lesbian, Bisexual, Transgender, and Questioning Adolescents." *Journal of Gay & Lesbian Social Services* 21 (2009): 189–205.

Ragins, Belle Rose. "Sexual Orientation in the Workplace: The Unique Work and Career Experiences of Gay, Lesbian and Bisexual Workers." *Research in Personnel and Human Resources Management* 23 (2004): 35–120.

Ragins, Belle Rose, Romila Singh and John M. Cornwell. "Making the Invisible Visible: Fear and Disclosure of Sexual Orientation at Work." *Journal of Applied Psychology* 92 (2007): 1103–1118.

Ray, Nicholas. *Lesbian, Gay, Bisexual and Transgender Youth: An Epidemic of Homelessness.* New York: National Gay and Lesbian Task Force Policy Institute and the National Coalition for the Homeless, 2006.

Reinisch, June M. *The Kinsey Institute New Report on Sex.* New York, NY: St. Martin's Press, 1990: 141.

Remafedi, Gary. "Suicidality in a Venue-Based Sample of Young Men Who Have Sex with Men." *Journal of Adolescent Health* 31 (2002): 305–310.

Remafedi, Gary, James A. Farrow and Robert W. Deisher. "Risk Factors for Attempted Suicide in Gay and Bisexual Youth." *Pediatrics* 87 (1991): 869–875.

Renna, Cathy. "Williams Institute Experts Comment on Department of Justice DOMA Decision." Williams Institute, February 24, 2011.

Rhodes, Scott D., Thomas McCoy, Kenneth C. Hergenrather, Morrow R. Omli and Robert H. Durant. "Exploring the Health Behavior Disparities of Gay Men in the United States: Comparing Gay Male University Students to Their Heterosexual Peers." *Journal of LGBT Health Research* 3 (2007): 15–23.

Riggle, Ellen D.B. and Sharon S. Rostosky. "The Consequences of Marriage Policy for Same-Sex Couple Well-Being." In *The Politics of Same-Sex Marriage,* edited by Craig A. Rimmerman and Clyde Wilcox, 65–84. Chicago, IL: University of Chicago Press, 2007.

Riggle, Ellen D.B., Joy S. Whitman, Amber Olson, Sharon Scales Rostosky and Sue Strong. "The Positive Aspects of Being a Lesbian or Gay Man." *Professional Psychology: Research and Practice* 39 (2008): 210–217.

Riley, Bettina H. "GLB Adolescent's 'Coming out'." *Journal of Child and Adolescent Psychiatric Nursing* 23 (2010): 3–10.

Roberts, Andrea L., S. Bryn Austin, Heather L. Corliss, Ashley K. Vandermorris and Karestan C. Koenen. "Pervasive Trauma Exposure among US Sexual Orientation Minority Adults and Risk of Posttraumatic Stress Disorder." *American Journal of Public Health* 100 (2010): 2433–41.

Rostosky, Sharon Scales, Fred Danner and Ellen D.B. Riggle. "Is Religiosity a Protective Factor against Substance Use in Young Adulthood? Only If You're Straight!" *Journal of Adolescent Health* 40 (2007): 440–447.

Rostosky, Sharon Scales, Ellen D.B. Riggle, Sharon G. Horne and Angela D. Miller. "Marriage Amendments and Psychological Distress in Lesbian, Gay and Bisexual (LGB) Adults." *Journal of Counseling Psychology* 56 (2009): 56–66.

Russell, Stephen T. and Kara Joyner. "Adolescent Sexual Orientation and Suicide Risk: Evidence from a National Study." *American Journal of Public Health* 91 (2001): 1276–1281.

Ryan, Caitlin, David Huebner, Rafael M. Diaz and Jorge Sanchez. "Family Rejection as a Predictor of Negative Health Outcomes in White and Latino Lesbian, Gay, and Bisexual Young Adults." *Pediatrics* 123 (2009): 346–352.

Saewyc, Elizabeth M. "Research on Adolescent Sexual Orientation: Development, Health Disparities, Stigma, Resilience." *Journal of Research on Adolescence* 21 (2011): 256–272.

Saewyc, Elizabeth M., Linda H. Bearinger, Robert Wm. Blum and Michael D. Resnick. "Sexual Intercourse, Abuse and Pregnancy among Adolescent Women: Does Sexual Orientation Make a Difference?" *Family Planning Perspectives* 31 (1999): 127–31.

Saewyc, Elizabeth M., Colleen S. Poon, Yuko Homma and Carol L. Skay. "Stigma Management? The Links between Enacted Stigma and Teen Pregnancy Trends among Gay, Lesbian and Bisexual Students in British Columbia." *Canadian Journal of Human Sexuality* 17 (2008): 123–131.

Saewyc, Elizabeth M., Carol L. Skay, Sandra L. Pettingell, Elizabeth A. Reis, Linda Bearinger, Michael Resnick, Aileen Murphy and Leigh Combs. "Hazards of Stigma: The Sexual and Physical Abuse of Gay, Lesbian, and Bisexual Adolescents in the US and Canada." *Child Welfare* 58 (2006): 196–213.

Saltzburg, Susan. "Parents' Experience of Feeling Socially Supported as Adolescents Come Out as Lesbian and Gay: A Phenomenological Study." *Journal of Family Social Work* 12 (2009): 340–358.

Sausa, Lydia A. "Translating Research into Practice: Trans Youth Recommendations for Improving School Systems." *Journal of Gay and Lesbian Issues in Education* 3 (2005): 15–28.

Savin-Williams, Ritch C. *Mom, Dad, I'm Gay: How Families Negotiate Coming Out*. Washington DC: American Psychological Association, 2001.

———. *The New Gay Teenager*. Cambridge, MA: Harvard University Press., 2005.

Schiappa, Edward, Peter B. Gregg and Dean E. Hewes. "Can One TV Show Make a Difference? *Will & Grace* and the Parasocial Contact Hypothesis." *Journal of Homosexuality* 51 (2006): 15–37.

Schiavi, Raul C. and Daniel White. "Androgens and Male Sexual Function: A Review of Human Studies." *Journal of Sex and Marital Therapy* 2 (1976): 214–228.

Schwartz, Erin Coale. "With or Against Us: Using Religiosity and Sociodemographic Variable to Predict Homophobic Beliefs." PhD diss., Indiana State University, May 2011. UMI (34539 20).

Scourfield, Jonathan, Katrina Roen and Liz McDermott. "Lesbian, Gay, Bisexual and Transgender Young People's Experiences of Distress: Resilience, Ambivalence and Self-Destructive Behavior." *Health and Social Care in the Community* 16 (2008): 329–336.

Shilo, Guy and Riki Savaya. "Mental Health of Lesbian, Gay, and Bisexual Youth and Young Adults: Differential Effects of Age, Gender, Religiosity, and Sexual Orientation." *Journal of Research on Adolescence* (2012).

Simari, C. Georgia and David Baskin. "Incestuous Experiences within Homosexual Populations: A Preliminary Study." *Archives of Sexual Behavior* 11 (1982): 329–343.

Solarz, Andrea L., ed. *Lesbian Health. Current Assessment and Directions for the Future.* Washington, DC: National Academy Press; 1999.

Sourander, Andre, Anat Brunstein Klomek, Maria Ikonen, Jarna Lindroos, Terhi Luntamo, Merja Koskelainen, Terja Ristkari and Hans Helenius. "Psychosocial Risk Factors Associated with Cyberbullying among Adolescents." *Archives of General Psychiatry* 67 (2010): 720–728.

Steele, Leah S., Jill M. Tinmouth and Annie Lu. "Regular Health Care Use by Lesbians: A Path Analysis of Predictive Factors." *Family Practice* 23 (2006): 631–636.

Stevens, Richard Allen. "Understanding Gay Identity Development within the College Environment." *Journal of College Student Development* 45 (2004): 185–206.

Storey, Kim, Ron Slaby, Melanie Adler, Jennifer Minotti and Rachel Katz. "Eyes on Bullying: What Can You Do?" Newton, MA: Education Development Center, 2008.

Struble, Corrie Barnett, Lisa Lindley, Kara Montgomery, James Hardin and Michelle Burcin. "Overweight and Obesity in Lesbian and Bisexual College Women." *Journal of American College Health* 59 (2010): 51–6.

Suicide Prevention Resource Center. "Suicide Risk and Prevention for Lesbian, Gay, Bisexual, and Transgender Youth." Newton, MA: Education Development Center, Inc., 2009. www.sprc.org/library/SPRC_LGBT_Youth.pdf.

Sullivan, Andrew. "Why Gay Marriage Is Good for Straight America." *Newsweek*, July 18, 2011.

Super, John T. and Lamerial Jacobson. "Religious Abuse: Implications for Counseling Lesbian, Gay, Bisexual, and Transgender Individuals." *Journal of LGBT Issues in Counseling* 5 (2011): 180–196.

Szymanski, Dawn M., Susan Kashubeck-West and Jill Meyer. "Internalized Heterosexism: Measurement, Psychosocial Correlates and Research Directions." *The Counseling Psychologist* 36 (2008): 525–574.

Tang, Hao, Greg L. Greenwood, David W. Cowling, Jon C. Lloyd, April G. Roeseler and Dileep G. Bal. "Cigarette Smoking among Lesbians, Gays, and Bisexuals: How Serious a Problem? (United States)." *Cancer Causes Control* 15 (2004): 797–803.

Tolan, Patrick H. "International Trends in Bullying and Children's Health." *Archives of Pediatric and Adolescent Medicine* 158 (2004): 831–832.

Toomey, Russell B., Caitlin Ryan, Rafael M. Diaz, Noel A. Card and Stephen T. Russell. "Gender-Nonconforming Lesbian, Gay, Bisexual, and Transgender Youth: School Victimization and Young Adult Psychosocial Adjustment." *Developmental Psychology* 46 (2010): 1580–9.

Ttofi, Maria M. and David P. Farrington. "Effectiveness of School-Based Programs to Reduce Bullying: A Systematic and Meta-Analytic Review." *Journal of Experimental Criminology* 7 (2011): 27–56.

Vaughan, Michelle D. and Charles A. Waehler. "Coming Out Growth: Conceptualizing and Measuring Stress-Related Growth Associated with Coming Out to Others as a Sexual Minority." *Journal of Adult Development* 17 (2010): 94–109.

Vreeman, Rachel C. and Aaron E. Carroll. "A Systematic Review of School-Based Interventions to Prevent Bullying." *Archives of Pediatrics and Adolescent Medicine* 161 (2007): 78–88.

Walker, Julian S. and Jenifer A. Bright. "False Inflated Self-Esteem and Violence: A Systematic Review and Cognitive Model." *Journal of Forensic Psychiatry and Psychology* 20 (2009): 1–32.

Weinberg, Martin S., Colin J. Williams and Douglas W. Pryor. *Dual Attraction: Understanding Bisexuality*. New York: Oxford University Press, 1994.

Wilkinson, Wayne W. "Religiosity, Authoritarianism, and Homophobia: A Multidimensional Approach." *The International Journal for the Psychology of Religion* 14 (2004): 55–67.

Wilson, Gregory A., Qing Zeng and David G. Blackburn. "An Examination of Parental Attachments, Parental Detachments, and Self-Esteem across Hetero-, Bi-, and Homosexual Individuals." *Journal of Bisexuality* 11 (2011): 86–97.

Wilson, Helen W. and Cathy Spatz Widom. "Does Physical Abuse, Sexual Abuse, or Neglect in Childhood Increase the Likelihood of Same-Sex Relationships and Cohabitation? A Prospective 30-Year Follow-Up." *Archives of Sexual Behavior* 39 (2010): 63–74.

Wood, Robert G., Brian Goesling and Sarah Avellar. *The Effects of Marriage on Health: A Synthesis of Recent Research Evidence.* Washington, DC: Mathematical Policy Research, Inc., 2007.

Wright, Lester W., Anthony G. Bonita and Patrick S. Mulick. "An Update and Reflections on Fear of and Discrimination against Bisexuals, Homosexuals, and Individuals with AIDS." *Journal of Bisexuality* 11 (2011): 458–464.

ACKNOWLEDGEMENTS

For their invaluable feedback, thanks to Michelle O'Grady, Stefan Koch and Mary Dohrenwend. For believing in me as a writer, thanks to Parul Sud, Susan Smith, Bob Fisher, Susan Wilson and Diny Cerulli. Thanks to my parents for their love and support: Clarine Dohrenwend and Bob and Ellen Stone. Last, but not least, thanks to my wife and son, Kim and Leo, for doing without me on weekends and evenings so I could make this book happen.